AF084831

RELATIONSHIP
(Motley of love, trust, and emotions)

RELATIONSHIP
(Motley of love, trust, and emotions)

"**Mutual faith and trust are strong pillars of human relationships.**"

R. K. MOHAPATRA

Anecdote
Publishing House

Anecdote Publishing House
E-35-A, E Block, Gali No. 2, Ganesh Nagar,
Pandav Nagar Complex, Delhi - 110092

Published by Anecdote Publishing House
Copyright © R. K. Mohapatra

First Edition 2023

ISBN: 9788195890781

MRP: ₹ 299.00

All Rights Reserved

"All rights reserved by the author. No part of this publication may be reproduced, stored in a retrieval system, or transmitted in any form or by any means, electronic, mechanical, photocopying, recording, or otherwise, without the author's prior permission.

Although every precaution has been taken to verify the accuracy of the information contained herein, the author and publisher assume no responsibility for any errors or omissions. No liability is assumed for damages that may result from the use of the information contained within."

Book Promoted and Marketed by Champ Readers Pvt. Ltd.

Layout and Cover by Anecdote
Printed in India

Contents

Acknowledgments ix
Preface xi

Chapter-1
Relationships: Basic Principle & Fundamental Processes   1

Chapter-2
Human Relationships   7

Chapter-3
Personal Relationships   24

Chapter-4
Sibling Relationships   47

Chapter-5
Mutual Trust in Interpersonal Relationships   55

Chapter-6
Social Associations & Relationship   67

Chapter-7
Role of social media in Human Life   90

Chapter-8
Economic & Political Relationships   105

Chapter-9
What Relationship Do You Have With Your Colleagues?   125

Chapter-10
Business Relationships   132

Chapter-11
Managing Stress in Relationships   143

*Dedicated
to the
People of India*

Acknowledgments

I thank my friends, seniors, and colleagues whose inspiration and encouragement made this book possible.

I thank and appreciate my family, especially my wife for her constant support in completing this noble task and making it a success.

Thanks to the IRCON family for their support and motivation for this creative work.

The focus of this book is on individual irrespective of age, leaders, statesmen, counselors, and political visioner especially the younger generation. I am thankful to the young ones who shared their views and thoughts.

Thanks to all my Facebook friends for their warm input and continuous support.

Thanks to the Editors for creative ideas and editing of this book and Anecdote Publishing House for publishing this book.

Regardless of sources, I wish to express my gratitude to all those who have contributed to this work.

Information collected from various sources was not always noted or available. Thus, it is impractical to provide accurate acknowledgments.

Preface

The complexity of human relationships is never simple to follow; it is an intricate lacework, but a lacework made of steel"

—Mignon G. Eberhart.

There is a strong relationship between "falling in love" and "living with love." Humans have a close bond with the natural world and its inhabitants. Relationships are based on places, people, events, and activities. As a result, the term "relationship" varies from person to person. People occasionally need to evaluate how money, location, and time relate to one another. You can refer to it as a need-based relationship or a commercial relationship. The only reason the world exists is to foster healthy relationships based on needs. However, human relationships are created over time with a need-based framework "with money" or "without money." The difference between the phrases "falling in love" or "living with love" may be temporary or permanent. Love your life while living a life you love. Because you want to live for the one you love, being in love gives your life meaning and inner strength. Love improves your health, vitality, and happiness.

Are you familiar with the proverb "No man is an island"? There is a real and direct connection between people and places. Humans are social creatures, and it takes a lot of effort to establish a relationship between two people in society. People have many relationships with culture, community, place, heritage, and other living things. Because it plays varied roles in different scenarios with different people, locations, and things, we cannot define the word relationship as exclusive without carefully examining, summarising, and explaining a situation and a location.

Nobody in this cosmos will be able to survive without a relationship. Therefore, love is a source of joy and kindness for human beings to develop loving relationships. It can be as simple as the relationship between a parent and child or between two siblings, or it can have complex emotions that prevail between neighbours or colleagues. Emotions are the best ingredient of love. If your emotion is very pleasant and strong about a person or things, you naturally love them whether it is men, women, animals, trees, buildings, roads, birds and all living creatures. So, love is not relation specific; it is your likes and dislikes and your emotions about objects or things.

A lack of faith and deterioration of trust amongst cherished friends and couples are two main issues that plague relationships nowadays. Most interpersonal issues are caused by people's tendency to look at the world primarily from their personal and distinctive perspectives. Most of the issues are unimportant and have no bearing on the inhabitants. They feature disagreements about the neighbor's dog and their children, payments to others, contributions to religious activities, and topics like other peoples' tours and travels. Because of these unnecessary arguments, the human mind tends towards depression and anxiety, and bad relationships arise in society. However, the loss of closeness, tension, and anxiety put a strain on your finances since they alter your spending habits. Ultimately, all the efforts go in vain and drastically spoil the family due to a bad relationship.

People start to think negatively, which increases the probability of divorce, separation, and relationship breakups without a valid cause. They go for a mediator, a man, or a counselor to resolve the relationship issues. Human relationships take a deeper and convoluted turn like the political relationship between two countries, either for trade purposes or for peaceful co-existence. With the advent of social media, the virtual interaction between two humans also needs a specific method of building virtual relationships.

This book explores sociological, psychological, and organizational human behavior to establish good human relationships. This book also aims to assist readers in managing the intense stress that comes with having relationships because conflict is unavoidable in human interactions.

CHAPTER ONE

Relationships: Basic Principle & Fundamental Processes

The exceptional significance of personal and professional relationships in contributing towards the overall well-being of human beings has construed the crux of the sociocultural evolution of humans. The need to gather relationships develops right from birth. Humans crave love, intimacy, and care in every facet of life, personal or professional. There reigns a constant requirement of approval of acts, getting valued, and cherished throughout life. However, human relationships are convoluted and quite difficult to understand and manage. The modern industrialized societies have brought further challenges in deciphering meaningful long-term relationships. A healthy human relationship has become more difficult to flourish, emphasizing personal enhancement, rapid adaptations to technological influences, and mobility towards own benefit.

Understanding how relationships are initiated, developed, and maintained or terminated remains one of human psychology's core focus. Research has explored the subtle influence of sociocultural evolution and cognitive, affective, and motivational variables in the relationship process. However, the scientific interest in the whys and hows of personal relationships is quite nascent. History of psychological studies, the various emotions of love, lust, hate, and envy were initially reserved for the literary world. Nevertheless, the last three decades have witnessed an explosive rate of research by social psychologists to demystify human relationships. Yet, the studies are found to be kept far from the mainstream research of social, cognitive, developmental, and clinical psychology.

It is difficult to correlate the theoretical and empirical advancements of the conceivable aspects of relational structure, like family, friendships, romantic associations, cyber romance, and the processes involved. Aggression, cognition, social support, and loneliness have added a whole new dimension to the traditional thread of research.

Evolution of Human Relationships

The sophisticated ability of humans to relate to each other has been the key to our evolutionary success while developing a highly complex yet effective social organization. The human species have evolved into a social animal. And the dawn of evolution began as the hunter-gatherer humans started working and living in close association with each other. Human relationships are initiated first between the intimately known others, members of the own family, and other associated small and immediate groups. The elaborate strategies that humans have employed to develop interpersonal skills have immensely helped develop our cognitive and mental abilities and, in turn, shaped our achievements as a civilization. In fact, our cognitive capacity to create and maintain complex relationships has been the glue to hold together families, groups, or society as a whole. On the same note, the 18th century introduced a distinct revolution in social relationships, thus adding new feathers to the science of human resource management. The traditional face-to-face society disappeared through several historical events, and human relatedness and social integration drastically changed. The ideology of liberated, self-sufficient, mobile individuals, freed from the restrictive philosophies of societal norms and conventions, took birth and eventually got expressed politically through many revolutionary and dramatic changes like the French Revolution, the American Revolution, and Industrialization. A motley of ideologies floated across borders, crossing the barrier of time, and there, human relationships got refined and reshaped in the pages of sociology.

The traditional setting of social relationships was small-scaled yet long-termed and stable. One's place in society was highly regulated and decided by rigid and already prescribed norms. The relationships were close-knit, and there was hardly any need to relocate from the group. However, with the industrial revolution there came a large-scale dislocation and mobility amongst the unrelated humans, which developed the technologies of mass production. Soon, the reassembly of massive and socially disconnected humans created a crucial consequence in the way humans interacted and developed relationships. In modern mass societies, most of the humans we encounter or interact with are strangers. The anonymity of humans and relationships is omnipresent. Mobility has reached a new level, so much so that any organization, personal, social, or industrial, is running through the support of a hundred unrelated, unacquainted humans put together.

Relating to each other, which was once a natural, automatic process confined within a small community, has now become uncertain and problematic, thus drawing much concern and reflection over the evolution of humans. The present setting is convoluted, and as most of the humans we are interacting with are not known intimately, relationship building and its maintenance have become increasingly difficult. Therefore, with the advent of mass societies, a whole new science of interpersonal relationships emerged in the scope of social psychology.

The intense face-to-face interactions that have been the essence of social cohesion are now on the verge of disappearing. In the present scenario, human interactions' indirect, impersonal, and disembodied structure is rising. We, humans, are now highly influenced by strangers, and our purpose of the interaction is solely focussed on our further development, both cognitive and materialistic. The geographic, demographic, and social mobility have designed the concept of impersonal but symbiotic relationships, which are beneficial to each other. Maintaining a stable and flourishing social relationship has gradually become a new challenge.

Developing the ability to construct accurate, reliable, and flexible symbolic cognitive strategies is critically essential for a successful and satisfying relationship. The analysis of evolutionary and socio-cultural factors and their influence on humans' mental and behavioral changes remain the focus while studying human relationships.

Over the years, the study of human relationships has encroached farther than mere interpersonal attraction. Humans develop their social interactions in three pivotal stages of life; infancy or early childhood, teenage, and adult. The three stages are distinct in the attentional foci and nurture different cognitive abilities and experiences.

Besides, personal relationships between husband-and-wife are forming only one aspect of relationship studies. The study of business, political, and human-nature relationships has opened new avenues of sociology research to supervise organizational behavior and devise strategies for the global economy.

With the growing interest in the cognitive orientation of social psychology, human relationship cognition has garnered much attention. A close analysis of evolutionary, social, and historical contexts leads to the accurate understanding of human relationships and, thus, helps in coping with relationship imbalance and stress. A multidisciplinary perspective towards love and sexual desires, developing a sense of security in a long-term attachment, creates a personal and social relationship.

Conclusion

Human relationships are complex and convoluted. Every element is interwoven yet adds a unique value to how we perceive human relationships. A massive and persuasive effort is involved in understanding the way of effective communication and how to get along with each other. Managing relationships is the first step in the ladder of conflict management. Healthy relationships ensure good decision-making skills, improved emotional quotient, and better physiological health.

The study of human relationships comes under the purview of multidisciplinary research wings, including sociology, psychology, human resource management, behavioral science, and organizational behavior. This book attempts to encompass a comprehensive study on the various factors impacting human relationships, different types of human relationships, and the effective ways to manage and maintain a healthy relationship, personally, socially, and in the sociopolitical environment.

CHAPTER TWO

Human Relationships

Awareness of the relationship between a person's behaviour and experience and the wider culture that shaped the person's choices and perceptions is the key to studying culture through sociological imagination.

— C. Wright Mills

𝒮ociological analysis of human interactions happens at both micro and macro levels, thus leading to different kinds of human relationships. A group of people living in a defined geographical location, interacting with each other on a personal and professional front and sharing a common culture from society. As a matter of fact, an individual's personal decision doesn't occur in a vacuum; rather, it is highly influenced by societal norms and the individual's interactions and experiences with the other members of society. Cultural patterns and social forces influence people to choose one over another—for example, marriage. In the US, marriage between two individuals is entirely a personal choice. While

8 Relationship

in India, marriage is highly dictated by societal norms. The caste system, social status, religion, etc., play a crucial role in matchmaking.

While following the diktat, we often forget that culture and the prevailing societal norms are the product of the people in it. As per sociology scientists, they are treating such abstract concepts as real with material existence leads to the birth of reification. Over the past decade, there has been a paradigm shift in personal and social relationships. Conflict of ideologies is rising, resulting in steep divorce rates. Women are now highly qualified, independent, and empowered to lead a life on their own. Single parenting is gradually making a normal place in society. Not only women but single fathers are also on the rise. Similarly, countries like the US, where same-sex marriages are legal, have seen many lesbian, gay, bisexual, transgender, and questioning (LGBTQ) community.

In the evolving world with the changing needs for education, housing, and healthcare, economic conditions and employment have played a huge role in the present scenario of human interactions. Interestingly, the cohabitation of single men and women has also found a new place in society. Opposite sex or same-sex couples are raising children outside marriage through surrogacy or adoption.

Individuals build a society, society builds a nation, and the hierarchy thus goes on. Every human interaction has a role in constructing the social structure. The German sociologist Norbert Elias called this process of simultaneously analyzing the behavior of individuals and the society that shapes that behavior as figuration. To clarify it further, let's consider the example of religious practices. A country predominantly inhabited by Christians has more churches and provides holidays and other benefits to Christianity. On the contrary, in India, where secularism is the key, every religion is given its due priorities and respect. Although the secular system in India creates a religious threat and weakens our national sovereignty due to external interference, we still accept and adopt it.

Several factors play a significant role in the present world of human relationships. Ingrained culture, rapid industrialization, automation, digitalization, and adaption of new technology have tremendously altered the outlook of personal and organizational relationships.

Relationships you are born with

There are things, people, choices, and episodes in your life you cannot ignore. We all have a mother and father. We may not be seen this beautiful world without them. They are your first and foremost family members with whom you connect as a fetus and a baby.

As you grow up, you realize the presence of your extended family. Those are your grandparents, uncles, aunts, and cousins. These labeled relationships are the ones you are given in advance. These people school your emotions, language, beliefs, culture, and upbringing.

We gather the fact that some kids are orphans. Their parents leave them at the orphanages for multiple reasons. In such episodes, the first family to trust kids is the nurse, sister, or father who cares for them like sincere parents.

If the foster parents adopt you, they become your extended family. Initially, such kids have difficulty adjusting to the new environment. With time, such kids adjusted to the environment of tenderness, love, and care. It's better for their mental and physical nourishment.

Relationships you make in this life

We know that you cannot choose your parents. They might be good or bad to you, depending upon your life in the current scenario. But God gifts us all with the ability to choose, attract, or repel. With that, you can choose and make multiple relations in your life.

Friends

As you grow up, you would find people connect with you through play, gossip, intellectual maturity, and usual likes and dislikes. These friends can be in your neighborhood, school, college, workplace, or anywhere you go for a short trip.

However, some friends are very close to your life, and some stick to you for life. They are your best friends. They know everything about your life. You generally share your ifs and buts with them. They know your inner personality and understand you and your values in society. These best friends might be entirely different from you. They might not look from the outside. But emotionally and from the heart, they would always be there for you. That's why they are your best friends. Best friends influence your behavior and lifestyle in your daily life. They can save you when you are in distress. You can share everything with your friends, and you can rely on them. Friends always support you, and sometimes they listen to you what you cannot communicate with your parents.

They are good listeners. They can help you in every aspect of your life.

These are the relations you make over a period using your time and honesty. But this goes both ways for its eternal survival. Maintaining your best friend's relationship is tricky because time distresses you and makes your life difficult. Trust friends can help you to continue a good association with your life. The real value of friendship reveals only when you are in a trouble or panic situation. The matter may be good or bad; you listen to your friends whenever they want to share feelings with you. You can overcome your friend's stress when they face a crisis.

Lovers

Life teaches us so many things. It happens when you grow old as a teenager or an adult. It might be so that you marry the one person who was your boyfriend or girlfriend from when you studied together. In a lifetime, you would have a lot of lovers.

As human beings, we all need a partner for our biological needs. Though, it's not mandatory. But when we are growing up, we go through hormonal changes in our bodies. It instigates us to like someone once or multiple times.

Sometimes, you end up being with one person for your whole life because of your rich culture and religion. It brings a good sign to society if both couples live together and end their lives forever. The relationship is sustained very pleasantly only with good emotion and inner physical needs. Once the state of emotion reduces, give-and-take relationships can exist between partners. Society has always taught us that take more and give less. A man and woman can live together only because of love, trust, and respect. Once that is over, it is very difficult for them to live together. If they stay in a room we can say that there is an adjustment between two partners where there is no relationship. We may say that it is one kind of business relationship.

It could be a high miracle situation in today's era. If you think you have that one person who understands you from inside and outside and would be compatible with you throughout life, you mustn't miss the chance with them ever.

Create intimacy and understand each other better to know your partner more. To build intimacy, you have to praise your love in front of others: your close relatives, friends, and society. It is a human tendency to feel good to overhear positive opinions from your partner.

You have to do small things such as cooking a favorite meal for your partner, shopping at the weekend, suggesting a restaurant for dinner, or showing a favorite movie to develop a very close relationship with your partner.

These small actions create positive vibes, build intimacy, and turn your bad relationship into good. To maintain intimacy with your partner, you have always taken care of your partner in every step of your life, which can change a bad relationship and make a good relationship in your life.

Idols

The idol in your life can be anyone who inspires you a lot. These idols can be celebrities, public figures, philanthropists, any Samaritan, or your parents themselves. They become your tether for you to move against the harsh realities of the world. You need such people in life to be your anchor to come out of hard times.

Neighbors

We often have amicable, funny, uncanny, and even weird relationships with our neighbors. But without neighbors, there would not be any community. Despite everything going wrong, the neighbors bring out a sense of togetherness, belonging, and festivities.

Enemies

Often, you do not choose your enemies. People simply find you unattractive and jealous of your success or confidence. Or, you might mess up with some intentionally, and then they consider you their enemies.

Having enemies in your life is not at all cool. But you won't know when someone is trying to plot against you. So, enemies teach you to be careful and trust people after carefully looking at their attitude towards you and your dear ones.

Impact of Culture on Human Relationships

Since the dawn of Homo sapiens, people have grouped into communities to survive. While living together, people share common habits and behaviors, specific methods of reproducing, and eating habits. From shopping to conducting marriage, every human behavior involves a chain of human relationships. In fact, human behavior has a lot to do in building relationships in both personal and global forums. The inherited culture designs an individual's behavior and perceptions and thus channels the skill of building relationships. In short, a good behavioral pattern hatches a better niche for relationships.

Every culture is distinct and has an impact of its own. There were times when two families mutually negotiated for a marital relationship. Gradually, the culture of choosing your life partner out of love set the new trend. And then, there persists the culture of 'mail-order bride,' like in Nigeria, which is like a vehement denial of women's rights. The same procedure also prevails in some parts of India by the Scheduled Tribe community in Odisha. While studying the impact of culture on human relationships, we come across Cultural Universals, which are the patterns or traits that are globally common—for example- celebrating birth, wedding, or mourning rituals of the funeral after death. Such common threads where humans interact with each other more for professional benefits impact the business relationships.

Anthropologist George Murdock was the first to recognize the existence of cultural universals while studying the kinships around the world. It is found that cultural universals often revolve around basic human survival-like finding food and shelter, around shared human experiences of birth and death and medical care. More recently, humans have migrated to different places and adopted the localized culture with the growing population and search for greener pastures. Murdock's further research supported the fact that personal names, language skills, and sense of humor bridge the emotional gap between humans and thus help build satisfying relationships. Humor has been found significant in easing tension and managing stress in every kind of relationship. Despite the basic need of humans to interact, cultural differences are far more prevalent than the universals. Analysis of language structures and conventional etiquettes reveal the global management of human relationships. For example, in Middle East countries, two interacting people are supposed to be very close while conversing. However, there is a concept of minimal personal space in the US while conversing.

We all humans are ethnocentric in some variables, which has a greater impact on developing global relationships. While discussing the impact of culture on human relationships, one must not forget the phenomenon called ethnocentrism, where one believes that his/her own culture or beliefs are superior to others. Ethnocentrism based on extreme religious beliefs has often hindered the global economy, and the best example resides in the current state of the Taliban.

A shared sense of pride for one's own culture is healthy enough to impose on others while considering the latter as inferior. Cultural imperialism is printed in golden letters on the pages of human history. The political relationship between different countries does carry a hint of cultural imperialism. European colonizers who traveled across the oceans in pursuit of transforming the uncultured savages had imposed not only their governance but also the dress codes, eating habits, religion. A more recent kind of cultural imperialism comes under the disguise of scientific developments. The introduction of agricultural methods and plant species of the developed nations to other countries while overlooking the indigenous varieties have become a new source of conflict in human relationships on a global platform.

Ethnocentrism has produced a stronger impact on older and more conservative generations as they confront the new advances in the culture. It is often called culture shock. A wide gap in mentality is common between two different generations. Often, sticking to conservative norms and delivering derogatory remarks on a newer mindset results in a bitter relationship. To combat such situations, anthropologist Ken Barger has propelled a thought of cultural relativism, which refers to the practice of assessing a culture by its own standard rather than putting it through a lens of the previously conceived notion. It is obvious to have conflicting ideas and differences in opinion. However, a balance in thought and action is essential to maintain any personal, social, business, or global relationship.

Contrary to ethnocentrism, xenocentrism is another phenomenon where humans tend to consider a different culture as superior to their own. Several socio-psychology studies have revealed behavioral changes in humans who went xenocentric. For example, students who went abroad and got inclined to a newer culture found it difficult back home.

It is certainly impossible for humans to keep their cultural biases at bay. However, to ensure a better relationship, it is essential to acknowledge the differences without imposing your thoughts. Sociologist Harold Garfinkel's breaching experiment is quite famous for analyzing social norms and conformity sociological concepts and has been used to study human behavior in social settings. A suitable example of this is the generalized response of the majority of society towards same-sex relationships. Society generally tends to veer towards homophobia in its outlook and refrains from prolonged interactions with gays and lesbians. It is primarily due to the concept of 'not fitting with established cultural notions.' However, to maintain the decorum of the ambiance, everyone remains amicable with each other, and peace prevails.

Why do we lose some people in our life despite a strong bond? The main cause is people need a change in their life; they want to be free from all obstacles, and after all, advancements in technology change their mindset from the conventional system in society.

You have already heard the phrase 'Change: the only constant aspect in life'a couple of times. That's real. People need space, talent, time, and emotions to evolve. If you do not change, others around will.

You cannot force them to stay with you. If you look around the world stats, there is a high rise in divorce, remarriages, deaths, births, and whatnot. It's just the attachment that hurts the most when people leave you for unknown reasons.

Sometimes:

- You know the reason, but you do not want to accept it.

- The person who leaves cannot tell you why you would find excuses for them to stay. That's not what the other person wants.

- You simply cannot accept that you are not enough for someone who is loved dearly.

Technological Interventions in Human Relationships

Staying in touch is the essential key to a healthy and happy relationship. If industrialization has led to dislocation from the closed one, the same technological advancement has paved the path of keeping in touch. Communication is put into a whole new dimension through the internet and smartphones. One can connect with anyone through a single click. Gone are the days of writing letters or waiting for the postmen to deliver a piece of telegram. The time is fast-paced and information is transmitted through an email or a WhatsApp message within a fleeting moment.

Nowadays, considering the modern digitalization and introduction of artificial intelligence in several aspects of doing business, human interactions are witnessing a magnanimous change. Finding a lost friend or getting in touch with a prospective employer everything can happen over a smartphone. Social networking sites like Facebook, Instagram, Twitter, and LinkedIn have opened new modes of connecting with people worldwide.

Digital technology has served as the steam engine for a new kind of relationship between employer and employee, organization and people in the information society. With the increase in the pace of innovation, there came a wide knowledge gap between generations. Technological gadgets that catch on quickly with one generation often dismiss an older generation's skepticism about the sudden change. For example, the customer support system of several organizations has implemented artificial intelligence by incorporating virtual assistants. While the younger generation finds it cool, the older generation complains about the lack of human touch and time consumption of the customer support system. The organization's support system changes very rapidly due to technological innovation.

Sociologist William F. Ogburn coined the termculture lag, which represents the elapse in time from introducing a materialistic change to its acceptance in the non-material culture. And this culture lag is increasing with the advent of newer technical updates now and then. For example, the government implemented Goods and Services Tax (GST) in 2017 by subsuming 37 different central and state taxes with ITC eligible across the value chain with the intention of One Nation, One Tax. After five years, about 1060 amendments were issued by the GST Council. The traders and business houses resist to accept the new system for the first two years, and after that, structural changes were accepted and now operate smoothly.

Although communications have been made easy, the digital world has snatched many aspects of maintaining harmony. The virtual world is illusionary and addictive in chorus. Mobile games have ruled out the very essence of socializing for younger children. Monetary affluence attracts younger breeds better than love and care. Screen addiction is a rising concern for the medical fraternity. Cybercrimes have encroached into a new dimension of identity theft, blackmailing, and sexual crimes. Political fabrication of human emotions has shaken up the whole foundation of communal harmony globally.

Conclusively, technology brings people together and has planted new seeds of separation and conflict.

Globalization Influencing Relationships

Along with the technical advances, the integration of the world markets has allowed a greater exchange of culture, thought processes, and innovative ideas through globalization and diffusion. Increased communication and air travel helped integrate several organizations and improved international relations. Doors of new businesses opened, which allowed the flow of finances, people, and technology. Many big conglomerates of developed nations hire workers from developing countries at a cheaper rate due to the advancement of technology applications in the workplace. The same rule applies to procuring resources as well. In one way, if this has improved the job market and financial status of developing nations, it also has implemented severe consequences. The best example is the racial crimes many Indians and Asians face in the US and Europe.

On the other hand, the process of diffusion refers to the integration of international cultures. The sudden surge of candle lights march in India, political outrage against one country's government in another country, and verbalizing LGBTQ rights across the globe are common examples of diffusion. The concept of 'Vocal For Local' and the vision of India Atmanirbhar Bharat Abhiyaan may be affected due to technological innovation and the low cost of foreign goods. With globalization came along the concept of 'think globally-act locally.' Human relationships are now more pronounced, refined, and open to acceptance and adjustments.

Conclusion

As viewed by conflict theorists, the social structure of human civilization is inherently unequal. The core theory of conflict in human relationships is the effect of economic production & service and materialism, the dependence on technology in the rich nations, and the lack of education in the poor.

An employer has always dominated the employee by nature. However, today employees (especially Millennials & Generation Z) challenge the employer regarding the terms and conditions of the service contract if it does not conform to the statutory requirement under the law. We should know that there is a service contract between employer and employee. The employees have to work and perform the job in terms of the agreement. It is the most challenging time for employees, irrespective of their organization/companies during this Covid era to sustain their service. It is also challenging for them to get a promotion or new employment in other organizations.

Despite economic uncertainty, the spending expenses of Generation Z (18-25 years) in terms of vacation are almost double that of Gen X and Millennials. The younger generation wishes to be free from moral, physical, or physiological restrictions. The perception and attitudes are different towards life between the generation. There is a huge gap between all the age groups in relation to service, spending, earning, buying a home and vehicles, and creating a retirement fund. As far as gender is concerned, the growth of understanding in service and other work in society is seen better in females than males.

The older generation is more concerned about healthcare and financial security. On the other hand, women voice their demand for equality in every domain. And then, society's material production system directly impacts human relationships on the global platform.

Human interaction is a continuous process of deriving meaning from the objects in the environment and the actions of other humans. From the hunter-gatherer stage to pastoral societies to digitalized life, human interactions have come a long way while incorporating a dynamic and fluid culture that helped nurture better relationship goals at both personal and organizational levels.

There has been a drastic change in the human-nature relationship and its impact on people's health worldwide during the past decades. The researchers, doctors, and environmentalists are worried about the nature-human relationship; we must be concerned about that. However, every step forward has caused a few implications too. Managing stress and conflict management are two key foci in sociological and psychological research.

'The relationship between rich and poor is similar to the relationship between infinity and zero. It depends on the comparison scale with our wants and requirements in life. If our income is more than our want, we are rich. If our wants are more than our income, we are poor. Thus, we consider ourselves rich as our wants are far less than our income. We have become rich not so much by acquiring lots of money but by progressively reducing our wants. If we can reduce our wants, we too can become rich at this very moment.

Anyway, richness and poverty is based on our needs, requirements, day-to-day thinking, and dreams. God has never created a poor man or a rich man. You have to judge the quality of the poor and rich in life. Nothing will satisfy you in the outside world. You have to search inside yourself to get the inner consciousness, the inner light, and peace.

The relationship between karma (work) and the attainment of inner peace is co-related. You must search for it again and again with your inner consciousness and fulfill it. Focus on the main objectives of your life. You will get it only you have to know about yourself. Nobody will help you with the attainment of your goal. All are searching the peace, but nobody knows where it is? You have power, money, prestige, and everything, but you have no peace.

The quest for peace is a million-dollar question. Everybody is running and searching for it.

Peace is an inner need of the human mind. Money, power, fame, respect, etc., may not bring you peace. All of these things combined will not bring about inner peace. You can find peace based on your positive thought and day-to-day karma. Your work (Karma) and meditation can guide and help you in the appropriate route to accomplish it.'

CHAPTER THREE

Personal Relationships

Personal relationships are the fertile soil from which all advancement, all success, all achievement in real life grow.

— Ben Stein

Introduction

While studying the social psychology of relationships, an interdependence theory persists in explaining the elicitation of emotions in close relationships. According to the theory of interdependence, close relationships are formed not only based on loving or liking but also, very often, in terms of dependency on one another for the desired outcome. The first relationship that we develop right after birth begins the thread of developing a Personal Relationship. The emotional connection with our bloodline grows further with regular interactions and is strengthened through mutual experience.

No relationship is static. Every relationship evolves with time, and to enjoy the benefits of a healthy relationship, we as humans must develop skills, gather information, inspiration, and require a lot of practice and social support. The social association or affiliation between two or more people comes under the purview of interpersonal relationships. Such relationships carry a different degree of intimacy, reciprocity, distribution of power depending on the kinship. For example, the degree of intimacy between married couples is different from that of the siblings.

Personal relationships are often regulated through custom, prevailing civil law, mutual agreement, and form the foundation of social groups. Such relationships are created while humans interact in social situations. The equitable and reciprocal compromise made in the context of social and cultural influences forms the premise of personal relationships.

Why must you seek any relationship in your life?

Humans have different needs. They can be emotional, social, physical, financial, and anything we do not know right now. Needs may vary from one person to another. People are always anxious to fulfilling all their needs. For that, they are always dependent partly or wholly on others. They have to maintain their business or social relationship to fulfill their needs.

Social needs

You have hundreds of thoughts, inspirations, ideas, and feelings in your head and heart. It would be best if you expressed it. Suppressing them would only be entirely harmful to you.

Social gatherings, meeting friends and families, catching up with them, talking to them for hours is what you need as an outlet for fulfilling those social needs.

When you gather around them, you can easily express your ideas, thoughts, and feelings. Moreover, you won't feel alone when you are in a crowd of people who get you. We can say that loneliness is the enemy of humankind. Without being social, no single human can survive for a long time. We are not made that way biologically.

Physical needs

Hugging, kissing, and having sex with a partner fulfills our physical needs. Even shaking hands, greeting someone, or simply leaning on someone when upset can meet your necessary physical needs.

People often go to the parlor or salon to get the massage done. Our body is directly connected to the emotional brain. We understand and fulfill our physical touch with the other person. Therefore, we often form a relationship, temporary or permanent based on physical needs.

Emotional needs

You would always need someone who can listen to you without any judgment. It is not possible if you live alone. You would then want to have best friends, a lover, or close family members around you.

This way, you can rejuvenate your emotional health from time to time. You can discuss any emotional distress with your trustable friend circle. They would always be there to uplift your mood. They know what sets you off and how to bring you back to the real world.

Nowadays, emotional needs play an important role in our daily lives due to our lifestyles, working behavior, and family relationships. The emotional need is in high demand when social distancing is demanded and regulated by governments across the globe. Therefore, when we have the emotional support of people around us, we fight pandemics and other battles like recession, unemployment, divorce, death, and layoffs slightly better.

Financial needs

We need to earn to survive in society. There's no denying that. Real money is the economy's driving force and an individual need for survival. Even when you are employed or an entrepreneur, you need to impress and work for someone else. Human need is unlimited. Money comes from other sources; we have to find it out. Without money, we cannot survive in this changing society. It would be best to come across as someone worthy of their money. That is when you earn and feel energized. That is how you form financial relationships with others.

The Lifespan of Personal Relationships

Relationships being dynamic, possess a lifespan like a living organism. Every relationship has a specific beginning, growth, and gradual termination. Psychologist George Levinger has proposed a model for relationship development that highlights the different stages of building any relationship. The natural development of any relationship has the following five stages.

1.
Acquaintanceship

Humans carry an incredibly diverse system in their social system across cultures, and interestingly, the diversity is quite outrageous at the individual level as well. Getting acquainted with someone is highly dependent on physical proximity, first impressions, or blood relations. The strong commitment to developing a long-term bond has several aspects to ponder: parental care, the physiological underpinning of love, cognitive effects, signaling properties, etc.

2.
Build-up

At this juncture of relationship progress, people develop trust and care for each other. Intimacy and compatibility, common goals, and familial and social influence determine the continuation to the next stage.

3.
Continuation

Mutual trust plays a vital role in the sustenance of any relationship. This stage is more prominent in parental bonding, within siblings, marital, or romantic relationships. This phase is relatively longer as compared to the previous two stages.

4.
Deterioration

Resentment, dissatisfaction, loss of trust, and betrayals are some of the major factors contributing to this phase. Not all relationships are bound to undergo this phase, but those who show signs of trouble enter the downward spiral and eventually end. However, relationship scientists have proposed several ways to resolve the conflict and re-establish the faith in continuing the relationship.

5.
End

Termination of a relationship can be natural or manual. While death is the most common form of a natural end, breakups and divorce are examples of the manual way to end a relationship. In the case of familial bonding or close friendships, death remains the usual mode of the end. Recent studies have shown that long-distance relationship causes an imbalance in mutual trust and remain one of the contributing factors to marital discord.

Evolution of Personal Relationship

The need to belong has been crucial for the psycho-biological growth of the human race. Considering Maslow's hierarchy of needs, humans constantly seek love (sexual or nonsexual), care and acceptance. Thriving under parental care is nothing but the need for safety. Similarly, coming out of an abusive marital bond underlines the need for self-esteem.

Every individual engages in a relationship that is rewarding in both tangible and intangible ways. As per the social exchange theory, relationships develop while analyzing the cost-benefit ratio. Individuals eye the rewards before investing in any relationship. It might sound crass, however, consider the example of arranged marriages. A good looking girl is sought for a fruitful marriage in the hope of reproducing good looking, healthy offspring. There prevails a universality in coupling and long-term relationships. Couple mate to fulfill their physiological need of sexual desires. The burden of raising a child is overlooked for the rewards; raising in social status with the child's achievements, receiving emotional and financial support in old age.

The effects of experiences in close relationships on the development of both favorable and unfavorable personality characters shape the attachment theory. The infancy of human relationships stems from parenting. The availability of a caring, supportive relationship partner develops the first sense of attachment security. This, in turn, helps in nourishing the self-esteem of both the partners, constructive coping strategies, maintenance of emotional stability and mutually satisfying relationship throughout life. An augmented sense of security has a great impact on mental health, social judgements, and interpersonal skills. Attachment theory substantiates the evolutionary mechanism of human relationships. The innate psychobiological system motivates humans to seek proximity to protective others in times of need. Most of the personal relationships are bound within the limits of a 'safe haven'.

Infants build the first kind of personal relationship with the primary caregivers; the parents. As we grow and go through different stages of childhood, adolescence, adulthood, we develop bonds with relatives, friends, co-workers, and romantic partners. Thus personal relationships come in various forms to us, with both sexual and nonsexual needs. While conceptualizing the normative aspect of attachment-system functioning, individual differences play a significant role. Interactions with attachment figures who are responsive at the time of need to promote a sense of security and build a positive working model for the relationship. When/if attachment figures are not supportive, a negative working model is built and attachment insecurities become more prevalent in the relationship.

As per the socio-psychological analysis of Bowlby, attachment insecurity for personal relationships has two components: attachment anxiety is worrying about the unavailability of the partner in the time of need and attachment avoidance is about developing distrust over the partner. Psychological analysis projects scores to understand human's attachment tendencies. One who scores low in both the parameters is considered as more consistent in maintaining a relationship for a longer duration. An adult's location in the insecurity dimension is assessed through questionnaires and coded clinical interviews.

Marriage and family are the two essential ingredients of building a personal relationship. Conservatively, marriage is defined as a sexual relationship between two individuals to procreate and maintain permanence. Over the years, human civilization has grown enough to sanctify a marital union legally. Several cultural beliefsand religious outlooks in northern Africa and East Asia still support the concept of polygyny, where a man is allowed to marry or have a sexual relationship with more than one woman. Statistically, only 1% of the world's culture carries out polyandry as well, where one woman is married to more than one man. The past few decades have seen a revolutionary change as cohabitation, same-sex marriages, and single parenting gained prominence.

Over the years, technological interventions in our lives have brought a drastic change in how we perceive personal relationships. Though humans have a better understanding of love and emotions scientifically, there have been many distractions. Work pressure, strangulating competition, and addiction to advanced gadgets have rather pulled us apart from building close human associations.

Types of Personal Relationships

1.

Parent-Child Relationship

Parenting is one of the most fulfilling responsibilities of human life. Along with joy, there come some huge challenges while raising a child. A strong parent-child relationship is essential for the overall well-being of the child as well as the parents. It ensures the physical, emotional, and social development of the child. This relationship crafts the basis of the child's personality, perspectives, life choices, and behavior. Young children who grow in a healthy ambience with their parents have a better chance to develop content relationships in future as well. It promotes the child's linguistic and emotional strength and makes the child capable of handling stress. Children under good parenting are found to have better academic skills.

Some of the key aspects of positive parenting are as follows:

- Every interaction with the child is an opportunity for the parents to connect well. Warm and loving gesturesand keeping direct eye contact encourage children to interact more.
- Children are naïve and need structural guidance. Setting a few rules does no harm.
- Empathise with children, if not mollycoddling. Lending an ear to their concern makes children trust their parents.
- Participative parents are good role models.
- Inculcate problem-solving habits in the child.
- A simple 'I Love You' works wonders for naïve minds. Good parenting starts with loving the child.
- Availability of parents at the need of the hour helps build attachment, security, and trust.

On a similar note, the relationship between adult children and their ageing parents carries considerable significance. Across cultures, filial responsibilities towards ageing parents have been a crucial dictate. There are many countries, like the US, that have a filial support law that imposes a duty upon adult children to support their impoverished parents and other relatives. In case the children fail to abide, nursing homes and other government agencies take legal action to recover the cost of caring for the parents. However, in countries like India, filial responsibilities are culturally ingrained. Families are more aligned towards patriarchy where the male child inherits the family name and carry forward the legacy. Sons remain the custodian of the parents.

In the past few decades, a whole new perspective has come up in the social upbringing of children. Additionally, there is a paradigm shift in the outlook as well. With evolving education and women empowerment, girl children are now capable and inclined towards taking care of their ageing parents. Out of love or respect or the sheer sense of responsibility towards the procreator, the child-parent relationship is maintained.

2.

Marital Relationship

As the generalized idea goes, a relationship between a legally accepted husband and wife is called a marital relationship. In most cultures, marriage vows involve implicit as well as explicit expectations of joint parental care. Both partners remain loyal to each other, showering mutual respect and love keep the marital bond intact for a long time. The benefits of any marital alliance are obtained through mutual commitments to each other and require a foreclosure to other attractive and distracting options.

With evolving time, love has found its role as a commitment device in marital relationships. Psychological studies by Hirshleifer have characterized the emotions that help people to defy immediate and seemingly rational self-interests. The emotion of love often makes people believe that they have found their soul mate amidst the billions of possibilities. Love provides genuine motivation to foreclose other options by providing an immediate reward or punishment. Those in love often proclaim over the extravagant display of loyalty; such as committing towards marriage, sacrificing career, or risking one's life. Expressing love through expensive expenditure has crafted its own niche in maintaining human relationships. These signals are hard to fake, thus serve as a strong motivation for continuing in the relationship.

In marital bonds, love is more often associated and also expressed through sexual desires and this desire to be physically close to each other motivates the relationship to continue. Additionally, as soon as a child is born, the responsibility to become an ideal parent captures the centre stage. There are several pieces of evidence where a marriage works out till the end just to secure a decent and harmless future for the born child.

3.

Romantic Relationships

Any human interaction or association can range from platonic to intimate with both positive and negative impacts. A modern terminology has evolved over the years, like 'in a relationship'. Such statuses signify the person being involved in a romantic relationship. Such relationships depict an emotional and physical intimacy with commitment and of course monogamy. Across cultures and amidst various conventions, romantic relationships can culminate into marriage or may remain as casual dating and even ethical and accepted polygamy.

Some of the basic types of romantic relationships involve:

a) Dating: This often starts casually to have fun together. Two people often get attracted to each other as mere infatuation, either physically or intellectually. Similar perspectives towards life, attractive facial features often cause infatuation. Dating usually starts on a casual note to check the potential outcome of togetherness. Two people initially attracted to each other might not end up being together forever. Thus, dating is a non-committal and explorative form of relationship.

b) Committed: In such a status, two people decide to be together in the foreseeable future. Apart from love, a mutual understanding works out between the two people involved. They tend to spend more time together and invest enough emotions to let the relationship mature positively for both of them. People committed to a romantic relationship are often given terms like boyfriend, girlfriend or partner. Many committed relationships get transformed into marital bonds. However, countries with strict religious and societal norms do nourish the concept of honour preservation. There are numerous cases of honour killing in countries like India and Pakistan where caste and religion play a crucial role. Moreover, in conservative societies, even today, choosing your partner on your own is considered disrespectful.

c) Live-in: A bridge between committed and marital status is considered a Live-in relationship. In such cases, two people are physically intimate, exhibit sexual intercourse, share accommodation, and familial responsibilities; however, they are not legally married. In countries governed by Islamic laws, live-in relationship is considered a crime to the almighty and is a punishable offence. In India, the situation is still nascent. Big cities like Delhi and Mumbai have seen a rise in live-in relationships while small towns still consider such kind of intimacy as a moral sin. However, in western countries, live-in is quite common and there are many live-in couples who have given birth to children outside the wedlock.

d) Casual: Generally, sexual intimacy does not crop up in a casual romance. People like each other, spend time with each other, and do not share any emotional intimacy in a casual relationship. It is short-term with no set goals to achieve.

e) Friends with benefits: This is a burgeoning phenomenon in the millennial generation. With no emotional connection or urge to get married, two people come together for casual sex. They might see each other often for just having sex or might end up having a one-night stand. Non-committal in nature, such sexual activities are more like satiating the physiological need rather than procreation.

f) Situationship: A romantic relationship that is not explicitly defined or committed is called situationship. DTR (Defining the Relationship) talks are often omitted from the interaction between the two people. But then, this is quite different from casual sex. There exists an emotional connect if not explicit romanticism or commitment towards each other. Two people like each other but not on the same page of mental set-up often end up in a situationship. When two people explore something, they develop a relationship; we may call it this relationship is developed based on the situation. New generation called is 'hanging out'.

g) Polyamory/Open: A person having multiple romantic and sexual partners is considered to be polyamorous or in an open relationship. Such relationships are mutually accepted and thus, it is often called ethical polygamy. There are no labels in such relationships. The partners can be committed, exclusive, or may be open.

Sternberg's triangular theory of love forms the framework of romantic relationships in human psychology. Love, passion, intimacy, and commitment are the four pillars of romanticism. Passion encompasses excitement and attraction within a relationship, while intimacy defines the degree of closeness. Commitment, on the other hand, oversees the decision to stay and nurture the relationship. Depending on their presence in a relationship, romanticism is classified further as follows:

a) Infatuation: Passion only

b) Empty love: Commitment only

c) Romantic love: Passion and intimacy

d) Fatuous love: Passion and commitment

e) Companion love: Intimacy and commitment

f) Consummate love: Passion + commitment + intimacy.

This often culminates in the desire for procreation.

A human mind is a complex machine. Not everything that runs in the conscience is visible on the outside. Human relationships are convoluted as emotional needs, financial security, and sexual desires channel our actions and perspectives in life. As romantic relationships do not revolve around any legal obligations, it becomes imperative for the partners to be transparent to each other to maintain a healthy ambience within the bond. One, involved in any kind of romantic relationship must scrutinize certain details. What does one want from the relationship? Is it future-oriented or casual or for only fun? The answers to these questions must be the same for the two people involved or planning to be involved. Hearing out the truth is always better than hatching assumptions.

As per sex therapists, 21st-century people are more materialistic and career focussed. Many suffer from commitment-phobia. On the same note, the world is changing. Survival instinct is more prominent than ever and one must gather the autonomy of oneself to flourish in any kind of relationship. The inner feeling of emotions plays two significant roles. Psychologist Tennov identified the experience of limerence or obsessional love. Intrusive thinking about the partner, acute longing for reciprocation, fear of rejection, intensification of feelings during adverse conditions, and high intensity of solo feeling are some of the essential ingredients of limerence. These make one ultra-sensitive towards the partner's actions and signals. Stating the true goals of every relationship, right at the beginning clears out the fog of imagination and expectation.

As the relationship develops, love relates to other experiences and promotes the relationship to grow or end. The feelings of connectedness, closeness, empathy, affection, and admiration serve as nourishment to a relationship. Biology, on the other hand, includes a whole array of neurotransmitters and hormones that carve the obsession for someone. For example, the amount of serotonin in a passionate love is quite equivalent to that found in patients suffering from obsessive-compulsive disorder. In short, the phenomenological and biological studies conjointly confirm that the emotion of love plays a significant role in the continuation of a relationship.

4.

Single Parent

Raising a child or children without a spouse or a live-in partner is defined as single parenting. Divorce, abandonment, domestic violence, rape, death of the other parent, or single-person adoption forms the structural basis of single parenting. The history of human civilization has witnessed several dreadful wars and plagues which contributed to the initial chapters of single parenting. Work accidents and maternal mortality during childbirth were common in the past. However, such single parenting was often short-lived as remarriages used to occur.

Over the years, domestic violence and adultery have caused a considerable number of divorces, leaving the child under the custody of the most suitable parent. In most cases, considering the child's basic requirement in the growing phase, the custody goes to the mother. Single mothers are more vulnerable to emotional attacks from society than single fathers. Very often, single mothers fall prey to mental health issues and financial hardships. Anxiety and depression, drug abuse and PTSD are common amongst single mothers.

Social reformer David Blankenhorn has elaborated the impact of single parenting on children in many of his books. Delinquency, drug abuse, school dropouts, teenage pregnancies are common in children raised by single mothers. These children often worsen in physical health behaviour and are continuously bullied by their peers. Children with no father show more discontentment and often engage in antisocial behavior and juvenile delinquency.

5.

Fragile Families

A kind of sub-category of single parenting, fragile families involve unintended pregnancy out of wedlock and sometimes rape. In such situations, the father is not completely in the picture and the relationship between the biological parents and the child is quite unstable. In most cases, the father does promise to raise the child, however, he leaves the scenario immediately or within a year. Such families often lack financial and emotional support and the child's psychological growth is quite hindered. Children develop a conflict with their parents and are more prone to crimes, suicide, and high-risk sexual behaviour.

6.

Parents by Choice

Many women, financially independent and emotionally strong choose to raise a child single-handedly. They are often called Choice Moms in western culture. Either by adoption or by surrogacy these women opt for parenthood.

Single parenting, whether thrust or chosen, is difficult. With none to share the decision-making process and financial duties, the full burden of parental investment is on the single parent. A lack of a second parent often distracts the child as he/she witnesses the normalcy of two parents in the surrounding. Inconsistency and instability in their emotional growth can be swept out by introducing a positive experience through the following-:

- Establish a routine and apply rules and discipline clearly and uniformly.
- Always keep in touch with the teachers, friends and others

who live in close association with the child.

- Do answer the questions about the other parent. Doubts are inevitable and the parent must respond calmly and honestly. An honest confession helps in giving the child more clarity towards his/her existence.
- Children must know the financial limitations and they must feel safe in your haven.

Understanding the Continuity in Personal Relationship

In the past, there has been a dichotomous view on the commitment towards the personal relationship. Either it was considered intact or broken. However, as time passed by and human lives came under the influence of several physical, demographical, emotional, and financial factors, a relationship between two people may morph from one type to another. For example, a romantic relationship between two people can transform into a marital bond and then can proceed through a divorce and still they can remain friends. The human mind often contemplates a relationship with alternative others and also forms alternate relationships with the current partner. The relationship type is characterized by the bundles of need fulfillment between people.

To demystify the changing morphology of personal relationships, let's take an example of a romantic relationship. During the initial days of courtship, Girlfriend X fulfills the emotional and sexual needs of Boyfriend Y. However, Y has now realized his altered sexual orientation as a gay and he needs X as an emotional companion than a sexual partner.

Similarly, the satisfaction one draws from one need fulfillment can often hinder the urge to quench other needs. There are phases in life when one has so engrossed within the friend circle and career-building that one overlooks the need for a romantic relationship. A new stage in personal relationships is emerging. To establish relational continuity, assessing and comparing the satisfaction attained in a personal relationship is vital. While acknowledging the fluidity in a personal relationship, human behavioral scientists have found that hardly any relationship is dissolved. Even statistical analysis of couples formally broken up raise question on the permanent dissolution of relationships. There are a couple who broke up but continued to have sex with each other, while there are some who maintain minimum courtesy but no hard feelings. Thus, the concept of relationship break-up is a misnomer and not consistent with the previous presumptions of dyadic relationships with prescribed trajectories.

Acceptance and Avoidance in Personal Relationships

There are several incentives one derives from close relationships- joy, laughter, love, and companionship. A study conducted by Kiecolt-Glaser (1996) proved a correlation between strong personal relationships and physiological markers of the cardiovascular system, immune system, and endocrine health. If our overall health is affected by our social ties, what happens to our bodies when the ties are disrupted? The threats in relationships, like, jealousy, conflict, rejection, and competition are inevitable. Every relationship is bound with pain which has some seriously detrimental effects on our body.

The repeated rejection or negative evaluation within a

relationship leads to increased cortisol production and ambulatory blood pressure. A direct threat to physical health remains permanent within abusive relationships. Despite the threats, humans are still motivated to establish strong personal relationships to ensure emotional stability. Little study has been done to understand the 'goal theory perspective' to establish and maintain a relationship. If a prospective relationship shows a chance of a desirable outcome, the motive is to Approach. And in case, the focus shifts to undesirable and punishing aspects, the motive is to Avoid. This Approach-Avoidance distinction provides the fundamental insight as analyzing the avoidance goals can prevent one from impending pain.

The Approach-Avoidance system is quite independent of each other. The presence of incentives in a relationship doesn't mean the absence of threats and vice-versa. On the same note, an individual's interpersonal goals have a greater role in shaping emotion, cognition, and behaviour. Studies by Derryberry and Reed (1994) showed that individuals with strong approach motives were inclined towards the gain, while one with avoidance motive queued up behind the negative aspects.

Advantages of managing effective relationships in life: Mental, social, physical,and emotional support

This book discusses multiple needs a human has for connecting with other humans. You meet all those needs one by one. That's when you have the most stable and trustable relationships in your life.

A boost to your productive side

Often, people can do wonders in their lives when they have

even single support to boost their creativity, originality, and talent. If you know that even a single person believes in everything you say or do, would you not do everything possible to surprise and impress them with your productive side?

Elevation of your professional life

Many effective relationships are necessary for the survival of your profession and business. Businesses are all about working with the people, for the people, and of course, by the people. It is all about how you manage, find, and hone the talent around you. So, when you have many effective relationships in your life, they all trust your word, work, and thoughts. Make the best use of it to grow in your professional life.

Development and recognition of your brand

Brand may be your favorite because you continuously work on that, and people recognize you on your brand name and product name. It educates you about the latest trend, thoughts, ideas, and how others live their lives around you or far from you. I want to share that 'I talk to multiple new people quite often'.

They all get to know you personally, even if you are exceptionally tremendous or bad at your professional level. Having effective relationships at a personal level is always a boost and space to recover from any loss in your life. It's the ultimate escape you can ever want from all the showbiz.

When people know you personally, even your name sells in the market. Not literally, but figuratively. You won't even need to use the name of your profession or business. You would need to recommend someone and get the work done. Your goodwill can impact thousands or millions of lives in this world.

That's the power of the ultimate management of effective relationships in your life.

Conclusion

The strongest emotions in life are sown during personal relationships' development, maintenance, termination, and reformation. An individual's interpersonal past always leaves its vestiges on the emotional tenor of every successful relationship. As the proverb goes, once bitten, twice shy. Every relationship experience in the initial years of life directly impacts the individual's behavioral pattern. Past relationships always transpire their effect during the intervening stages of social development. Identifying the origins and profile of emotions experienced within a relationship is imperative to understanding personal relationships completely.

CHAPTER FOUR

SIBLING RELATIONSHIPS

They outlast marriages, survive the death of the parents, and resurface after quarrels that would sink any friendship. They flourish in a thousand incarnations of closeness and distance, warmth, loyalty and distrust.

— Erica E. Goode

Introduction

The study of sibling relationships has a unique contribution to the scope of close or personal relationships. The most important aspects residing in sibling relationships are the emotions of constant comparison and competition. The constant scrutiny of physical attractiveness, abilities, or personality like aggressiveness, friendliness, etc., nourishes the sense of competition within the siblings, thus affecting the relationship in both positive and negative ways. However, this sibling comparison is unavoidable, given the non-volitional nature of the relationship. Moreover, the self-schemata based on these comparisons begins early in life and goes on throughout. There are psychotherapeutic cases where individuals are diagnosed with impoverished self-esteem caused by self-evaluative strategies. With the magnitude of complications and variations involved, this separate chapter is drawn exclusively for analyzing sibling relationships.

The Quirks of Self-Evaluation

The renowned psychologist Abraham Tesser has proposed a self-evaluation maintenance model (SEM) to study the comparison and competition in a relationship. As per SEM, siblings' response to comparison on various factors, namely, their performance, closeness in the relationship, and the relevance of the compared concept. To understand this phenomenon, let's assume two siblings where one is a chartered accountant and the other is an established scientist. Considering they are quite close, the accountant sibling won't be affected much by questioning his scientific acumen as that comparison is futile. Thus, the relationship in such a scenario is not adversely affected. However, if the scientist sibling is struggling with his finances, a comparison with his accountant sibling will draw much rivalry. A sibling will have a stronger negative response when outperforming the compared sibling.

A major cause of jealousy between siblings is social comparison through parental favoritism. Being outperformed often evokes defensive attributional strategies. As the threat increases with the closeness of the relationship, so do the SEM negative reactions. Friction is further aggravated if a younger sibling outperforms.

Apart from comparison, the other aspect of the SEM model is called reflection. It refers to the individual's self-evaluation being strengthened by associating with the accomplishments of the sibling. For example, the established scientist is proud of his CA brother for clearing one of the most difficult examinations. Such a situation arises when the self-relevance is low, and the sibling's achievements help in self-enhancement.

A further extension of this study focussed on the performance ecology siblings often develops to protect each other. The pair assumes specific roles and craft their niche by choosing divergent career goals. Downplaying one's achievement or concealing the other's failure has also been seen as a strategy to preserve harmony.

Downplaying the Importance of One's Success

The central premise of sibling relationship studies focusses on this attempt to downplay one's success if one has outperformed someone very close or loved. It is a way of preserving positive self-evaluation during failure and boosting it during success.

- Adolescent Siblings: They downplay their success in low-relevant tasks, while on high-relevant tasks, they downplay their failures. Regarding age, the older siblings often downplay their failure when outperformed by the younger ones. At the same time, the younger ones are often more protective of the self-evaluation need of the older sibling.

- Adolescent Twins: The downplaying mechanism is often guided by the performance and relevance and has less to do with their closeness.

- Young Adults: Downplaying success has more to do with empathy and concern towards the success, while in the case of failures, downplaying is done to bolster one's self-evaluation. Similarly, in the case of young adult twins, the downplaying mechanism is more prominent over worse performances.

Winning has always imparted a stronger effect on continuing a high-relevant task. Older twins and siblings, especially males, continue to perform irrespective of the outcome. Younger siblings often give up on activities. In the case of twins, they refrain from doing similar activities, presuming the risk of competition and comparison.

Effects of Relationship Quality

Positivity and self-esteem are mediated through the relationship's warmth, conflict, and parental partiality. Depression is a common side-effect of a bad ambiance during growing years. The relationship between siblings is strongly determined by the psychological adjustments one does within the relationship. Parental favoritism has a greater impact in the case of monozygotic twins than non-twins.

For relationships high in warmth, negative performance's effects on emotional reaction are less significant. Self-esteem improves in less conflicting siblings. In short, it is a vicious cycle where a healthy sibling relationship is maintained with accurate psychological adjustments. Decades of research have implicitly described the dynamics of the sibling relationship. Parents and family must acknowledge the psychological tendencies of older and younger siblings to give both of them a healthy ambiance to grow. The younger ones must not be deprived of the number of chances given to them to perform. Focussing on various factors like age, mental abilities, and physical strength help in realizing the significance of sibling bond when self-evaluation is threatened.

Biological Factors Influencing Sibling Relationship

1.

Birth Order

Birth order tends to play a part in reactions to competition and comparison, even for twins. In the case of adolescent siblings, the older siblings are more positive and less negative when outperformed over low-relevance than on high-relevance tasks. Older siblings who are outperformed by their younger siblings on high-relevance activities react more negatively than the younger siblings when outperformed by their older siblings. Although the more sanguine reactions of the younger siblings depend on the age difference, the effect is similar for twins where the age difference is inconsequential. Younger twins often find it easier to bask in the reflected glory of the older twin.

Birth order is an important aspect of a sibling's social identity. Younger twins may cope with their poorer performance by attributing the superior performance of their twin to their older age. In addition, as with sibling relationships, being outperformed by one's younger twin seems more damaging to the older than the younger member of the dyad. In case of the young adult twins, only the older twins who are insecure in attachment reacted negatively once they outperformed by their younger twins.

Behavioral science research by Beck, Burnet, and Vosper (2006) has reinstated that older sibling tend to be more dominant while the younger siblings are more prosocial and, presumably, less achievement-oriented. Younger siblings are also less positive about outperforming their older siblings on activities highly relevant to the older ones. They perceive their superior performance as potentially damaging to the sibling bond and feel empathy for their older sibling. The finding reinforces the possibility that younger siblings had always downplayed the significance of their success when they outperformed their older siblings on tasks of high sibling relevance, suggesting that the younger siblings are protective of their older siblings in this context. It also seems that the superiority of the older sibling is taken for granted by both members of the sibling pair.

2.

Niche Building

Older siblings and twins are more likely to continue engaging in activities high in self-relevance. It is more relevant, especially if they are males. Older siblings seem to have more power in the relationship than their younger siblings, while the younger siblings tend to cede even in the areas that are highly self-relevant. These younger siblings are likely to find other areas of activity that do not involve competition with their older siblings, which is described as the niche-building or performance ecology.

3.

Sex (Physical Activity)

There are a few differences observed with respect to the sex of the sibling pair. Male, but not female, adolescent twins are found to be more negative reactions when competing with their twin rather than with their friend. Thus, it confirms that the male twin dyads are particularly competitive with each other. This finding was unrelated to birth order. In the case of the young adult non-twin sibling sample, the expected three-way interaction of performance, closeness, and relevance on positive reactions occur only for the females.

Females are more positive when they perform better than their siblings than when they perform worse than their siblings or friend on high relevant activities. This confirms the emotion of empathy for the sibling over their friends. The same rule applies in the case of low-relevant tasks also.

4.

Zygosity

In the case of twins, monozygotic tend to be more positive in situations of competition than the dizygotic, suggesting that the monozygotic see their close relationship as buffering against the problems of competition and comparison. Alternatively, perhaps they are so similar genetically that situation of comparison and competition are less salient.

Conclusion

The socio-psychological analysis of sibling relationships provides an interesting insight. The main focus explores their reactions to competition and comparison, a ubiquitous aspect of their daily lives. There is convincing support for both the SEM Model and the Extended SEM Model, which highlight social and biological factors involved in improving the relationship quality. Still, there remains room to study the attributions siblings make for their performance and how they react to success and failure while interacting with their sibling or twin. Focussing on the relationships of twins and siblings provides important information about how these relationships work, particularly when social pressures threaten the personal bond.

CHAPTER FIVE

Mutual Trust in Interpersonal Relationships

Most good relationships are built on mutual trust and respect.

— Mona Sutphen

Have you ever wondered why or how a child enjoys it when parents throw her/him in the air? The child giggles as he/she relishes the time spent with their loving and caring parents. Why? The answer lies in the previous line itself. Love and Care! And a much bigger role is played by TRUST. A child trusts his parents. He knows that no matter what, his/her parents will catch him/her and won't let him/her fall.

Similarly, elderly parents nurture trust in their grown-up children that they will be cared for during their old age. In a love relationship or a marital bond, love may wane over the years; still, the relationship prospers with mutual trust. Any personal, social, business, or political relationship can blossom to a fruitful outcome only on the foundation of trust. Building and maintaining mutual trust is essential in every kind of relationship.

"Mutual faith and trust are strong pillars of human relationships."

As the saying goes, trust takes years to build, seconds to break, and an eternity to repair. Neither is it easy to develop trust in a relationship, nor is it difficult to let it wander. There is a close-knit relationship between trust and love. Trust begins with self. Trusting your judgments paves the path to trusting others. Trust is something that begins with truth and ends with truth. There is no other way to build a strong relationship without lending the concrete of trust. Any relationship that lacks trust or loses trust in due course of time shall eventually fail, and no one can save it.

Trust also plays an important role in the organization. Every employee working in a sectionor group does better work only if trust exists between the colleagues and higher and lower management. A leader can achieve success only if he /she believes their employees and works together with full trust. Hence, mutual faith and trust not only grow your family relationship but also develop a business relationship positively.

Why do you think divorces happen? Why do you think romantic relationships come to an end? Invariably, the answer revolves around trust. Mutual trust makes the partners feel secure and safe within the bond. Once the trust declines, every relationship goes through emotional anxiety and physical torture. Of course, the level of anxiety and pain depends on the type of relationship and the depth of emotions one has invested in it. In the case of short-timed relationships, where partners are not serious towards each other, not much pain is mustered.

The first step to influencing people is to gain their trust. Trust is the glue of life. It's the most essential ingredient in effective communication. It is the foundational principle that holds all relationships. It is a famous quote by American Educator Stephen Covey, which he often delivered in his self-help, and motivational classes. A trustworthy leader or speaker gets more attention than anyone else. If effective communication makes the essence of a good relationship, trust makes the concoction of effective communication.

We, humans, are bound to develop relationships, and while doing so, we nurture the different aspects of our emotional and physical well-being while churning out the whys and hows of love, care, and trust. Let's have a detailed look at mutual trust in interpersonal relationships.

Who Do We Trust?

Trusting someone is about offering our vulnerability to them. And we do that ideally with family, friends, and co-workers in our inner circles. As a child, our journey with trust begins with our parents first and then with close family members who closely associate with us. For example, grandparents, siblings or uncles, etc. Similarly, as we grow, we are taught to trust police officers, clergy or priests, and doctors or similar people who hold authority in life. However, education and personal experience in life play a vital role in shaping our trusting abilities. For example, encountering a single corrupt police officer can shape our perceptions of the whole police force. Similarly, we are taught to believe doctors as next to God, but our faith in them is slowly degrading as we find them doing unscrupulous business to preserve our health.

Trusting our parents is an inherent quality amongst us. No matter how rich or poor the parents are, every child trusts their parents' abilities to guide them. However, as we grow old, formal education widens our knowledge and develops our ability to decide for ourselves. Still, losing trust in parents and their parenting skills is extremely rare. On the same note, letting youngsters know about their Spidey-Sense of detecting a lie or danger is an important parenting skill. When children have go-to people, whether in their family or extended community, they are more likely to trust and with good reason. An individual's outlook, social behavior, emotional perseverance, and physical conduct are crucial to project him as trustworthy.

Trust In Parent-Child Relationship

With little to no training, a steep learning curve, constant failure, and punishing hours, parenting is the toughest job on this planet. And building trust is essential as well as a Sisyphean task for a parent. The emotional intelligence of the parents shapes their ability to develop trust with their children. Parents must practice trusting their gut feeling, take emotional responsibility, and balance trust with expectations.

These factors craft the frame for a healthy relationship between children and parents. Trust is created through a series of positive interactions between a parent and child, right from the stages of infancy. A trust created by the parent/child relationship is situational and has a lifelong impact on a person's ability to connect with others. As stated in earlier chapters, children growing up in a positive and encouraging atmosphere develop a better outlook on the world.

When kids are young, the emotions of both the parents and children often loom large, and such big emotions are disruptive and even obstructive. Parents are stressed between their personal and professional chores while juggling children's demands. To ease the situation, parents are often inclined to bribes, threats, and distractions. However, all such steps are temporary measures to adjust to the child's tantrums. The most crucial step is to increase their emotional literacy. The three tips for integrating emotional literacy are as follows:

- Acknowledge the child's emotions and ask the child to describe how he/she feels?
- Validate their emotions.
- Once they comprehend the problem, the parents must participate in solving the problem.

When parents teach children to take responsibility for their own emotions, they help them understand the parent-child relationship.

Emotional responsibility is the idea that each of us is responsible for how we feel and handle our feelings.

Every relationship works out by leveraging our expectations. A child expects the parents to give time, love, and care along with other materialistic gifts. Similarly, parents expect their children to do well in life, matching their education and lifestyle standards. In this process of expecting and delivering, both parents and children blissfully forget that they belong to a different generation. Their needs are varied from each other as they perceive life through different lenses of the time. Let's analyze the concept by this example.

Seventeen-year-old Aniket once asked his dad if he could go to the movies with some friends. His dad initially said no, but later asked him to decide on his own. Till that day, Aniket had never decided anything for himself. He just knew that a right answer makes his dad happy, and a wrong answer upsets him. Sure enough, when Aniket decided to go to the movies, his dad was disappointed in his decision.

What do we learn in this case study? When we give our teens the power to make a choice, we have to be okay with the ultimate decision, even if it's not what we had hoped for. To ensure that their decision is acceptable, make sure that you are okay with all options on the table. Parents have to limit their choices until they are confident in their decision-making. If Aniket's dad was not going to be okay with him choosing to go to the movies, then he should not have asked him to decide.

Secondly, parents must practice empathy when it comes to expecting teens to think through their consequences. They must help teenagers apply consequential thinking, which is the concept of weighing pros and cons, long-term vs. short-term, self vs. others, etc., in a decision-making process. In this practice of balancing boundaries with freedom and expectations with acceptance, parents build a strong foundation of trust. Perhaps, if Aniket and his dad sat down to talk about the consequences of each option, Aniket would have been better equipped to make the choices.

Helping kids navigate through adversity is one of the most difficult things to do as a parent. For most parents, the natural instinct is to step forward 'to show them the way' or 'prevent them from falling. 'When parents rush to help, prevent mistakes, or ease the pain, they deprive children of learning to trust themselves and solve their problems. Children perceive such behaviors as parents distrusting them.

Building Trust with Teenagers

As children grow older and become more independent, it can be difficult to find the balance between a teenager's need for independence and privacy and parent's need to know what's happening to keep them safe.

The child needs their parents' trust to help them in their transition through to adulthood. However, this trust needs to be mutual. Remember that the more this mutual trust is tested, the longer it will take for the child to feel confident with the parents. A relationship without trust leads to second-guessing and questioning each other's honesty. When your child was young, they probably trusted you unequivocally as the person that kept them safe. However, as children grow up and become more independent, they start to notice and question more. Around this time, the child may notice whether parents do what they proclaim, which is a key factor in building trust. Parents can't demand trust. It's a gradual process that requires mutual commitment and will inevitably strengthen the parent-children relationship. It shall also set children up to develop healthy relationships in the future. It's worth noting that teenagers are going through an intensely private time in their lives. Personal space becomes very important to them, so the desire for privacy doesn't always mean untrustworthy activity is taking place.

By building a trusting relationship with the teenager, parents are likely to see many benefits, including:

- Your teenager feels open and comfortable talking to you about difficult things.
- Your teenager demonstrates positive, trustworthy behaviors in other aspects of their life, setting them up for positive relationships into adulthood.
- Building a relationship with your teenager that goes beyond a parent-child disciplinary relationship and strengthening your bond for years to come.

Parents have to talk about the importance of honesty and trust; however, the same thing must also be reflected in the parents' actions. If a child repeatedly breaks trust without showing any signs of remorse, or if they show self-destructive behaviours, it might be time to seek a counsellor or psychologist, as this could indicate other underlying issues.

The Paradigm of Building Trust

Brene Brown, the famous American professor and author uses the acronym BRAVING to describe the paradigm of building and maintaining trust.

- Boundaries: Setting up parameters for what you will and won't permit in your life. We all have a bubble of comfort into which we allow some people and from which we hold others at bay. We have the right to say yes to what we want and no to what we don't want without guilt.
- Reliability: Knowing that we can be counted on to do what we say and say what we mean.
- Accountability: Owning up to our feelings, words, and actions, rather than blaming others.
- Vault: Holding our tongue and only sharing information that is ours to share or that we are given explicit permission to tell others if it is another person's story.
- Integrity: Living according to our values.
- Non-judgment: Speaking our truth and allowing others to do the same without making them or ourselves wrong for it.
- Generosity: Assuming that the other person has our best interest at heart and vice versa.

Trusting Your Partner

The very emotion of trust allows us to navigate the uncertain and complex world we live in today. With the rise of the internet, mobile phones, email, chat, and social media, it is much easier for people to connect or spend more time with co-workers than with family or significant others. Trust is integral to happy and fulfilling relationships in both our personal and professional lives. We require trust to develop over time to build successful and meaningful partnerships.

Relationships often break due to financial stress, communication difficulties, different mindset, and lack of trust. Authentic trust involves moods and emotions, trusting in ourselves and our judgments, trusting others, and the ability to forgive when agreements are broken. People cannot build trust if one person is willing and the other is not.

Two people sharing a successful relationship will demonstrate trust in a number of ways, like:

- Listening and supporting each other.
- Showing consideration and care.
- Trusting each other that you know what is best for yourself.
- Showing mutual respect for boundaries.
- Being dependable for the other person.
- No matter what comes up, you can feel safe.
- Resolving conflicts in healthy ways.
- The matchup between words and actions.
- Not controlling or monitoring each other.

- Trusting each other no matter where they are or whom they are with.
- A tight, strong bond.

When a couple has built a solid partnership on trust, they are free to be their authentic selves. Gaining trust takes time, and trust is a choice. Life is full of uncertainties, and if one has been hurt, either in the past or with the current partner, where the trust has been broken, one must continue trusting one's own instincts. It is common for one person to transfer their lack of trust onto a new partner for fear that history will repeat itself. In case one is stuck and feels that one cannot even trust one's own judgment, then it is the right time to seek professional counselling – and perhaps not the time to start a new relationship.

Conclusion

You know who you are. Can you try to know the real facts of your life? You are a strong man. You are a bad or a good man. You are a lovely person. All these adjectives about you people are saying. You know what you are. Nobody can describe you better than yourself. They only penetrate you based on your work, behavior, and momentums.

Not even your partner can pierce you because s/he can know about your outer picture. On the other hand, you know about your inner consciousness. Try to know very closely about your inner feelings and inner consciousness.

Be truthful to yourself. Don't blame others for any activity or event. Destroy your mental image because it is a vital cause of your worries.

Trust and time in the relationship bring happiness and honesty. Without trust, you may not build a long-term relationship with anyone. Trust in each other opens a path for open communication. You communicate openly with your partner and build a strong emotional connection in your life. To maintain a healthy relationship, you must spend quality time with your partner and communicate openly with full trust. You will feel good in your life and overcome all bad times as happiness will flourish in your life due to unconditional love and mutual trust.

Trust leads to acceptance of a relationship. As they say, love may be blind, but trust is never. A man's actions project him as trustworthy or not. Developing trust towards a person or social atmosphere highly depends on our educational background. Atheists form the best example of developing trust. People who believe in science and deny the existence of God define how education can influence one's trusting capabilities. One's ability to trust is influenced by age, personal experience, and preconceived knowledge. As we grow older, our cognitive abilities develop, and we tend to trust our judgments and depend less on parents or elders to decide for us. Trust is essential while developing interpersonal, social, or business relationships.

CHAPTER SIX

Social Associations & Relationship

He who is unable to live in society, or who has no need because he is sufficient for himself, must be either a beast or God.

— Aristotle

Introduction

Human life is communicative. We all strive as actors to negotiate our contradictions with each other amidst the social organization. From the hunter tribes of Andaman Nicobar Island or the tech-savvy humans of Japan, every human is a part of a distinct society with its own culture, tradition, and way of living. Human behavior and expression and management of emotions in the outer world play a significant role in shaping our social relationships. While parents form the first kind of close relationship, our social circle initiates first through playmates as a toddler. Soon, school and college life widen our circle. Friends, neighbors, colleagues, and work acquaintances form our social associations and have significantly contributed to developing our moral and social ethics as a human.

No man is an island. Have we ever wondered about the meaning and significance of this famous English proverb? Consider the pleasure of meeting friends for a get-together or talking to an old colleague over the phone. Every step one takes in grooming the social relationship, one moves a step closer to emotional well-being. It all revolves around one's perspective. Emotions towards a romantic partner are different from the emotions one invests in a friend. Many friendships break when a romantic relationship enters into life. Managing time between interacting with friends and a lover is difficult in many scenarios.

Similarly, the sociological aspect of organizational behavior reflects the harmony and acrimony between two competing colleagues. A common saying in the corporate world is that Colleagues can never be friends. However, over the years, many organizations have made sure to maintain a healthy atmosphere at the workplace. Flattened hierarchy in the organizational job profile has a tremendous effect on developing harmonious social relationships. A symbiotic association targeting an organization's ultimate goal has become the workforce's new focus.

As communication forms the primitive structure of any social relationship, we must understand the implications of good communication skills. While we babble with our friends and make a random call to a relocated neighbor, it is not an inconsequential aspect of our life. Rather, such communications help us accomplish the existence of the relationships and also let us learn the new rules of relating.

Evolution of Social Interactions

Besides the usual definition of society, sociologist Gerhard Lenski has highlighted the technological sophistication of society. Every invention by humans has led to a technological alteration in society. A society that encompasses elementary usage of technology depends on environmental changes. Highly industrialized society has more impact on the culture, thus adding new feathers to human organization.

Societies are classified within the spectrum of industrialization as preindustrial, industrial, and post-industrial.

Preindustrial Societies: Preindustrial societies have evolved from hunter-gatherer tribes to pastoral and then to horticultural types. Humans joined hands in sharing the work labor and divided the outcome. While hunter-gatherer societies entirely depended on the resources available to stay alive, pastoral societies included human interactions in breeding livestock, clothing, and transportation. As the pastoral societies emerged, specialized occupations started, and humans had to interact and focus more on a win-win situation. The barter system came to the rescue. Horticultural societies developed as a hybrid of both pastoral and hunter-gatherer. Humans gathered to grow their own food in a place where rainfall was adequate. Nomadic life stopped, and humans started living in permanent settlements with more stable and continuous human interactions.

As humans evolved to develop tools, horticultural societies transformed into agricultural types. Around 3000 BC, humans comprehended the science of crop rotation, soil fertility, and producing manure from waste. With better harvests and food surplus, human settlements grew into a town with more options for trade and commerce. At this stage of human evolution, humans were engaged in more contemplative and thoughtful activities. Music, literature, and philosophy became an integral part of human lives. Craftsmen designed the new dawn of civilization. With more leisure time and scope for humanities, creative writings, and decorative objects joined human interactions. With resources growing, social divisions too took birth. Humans could afford more resources from the higher stratum of society and declared the nobility. The division between men and women was more pronounced, and ownership of resources became a major concern.

Following came the feudal era, which showcased the power hierarchy. Nobility bestowed one with the power of ownership of the lands, and less powerful peasants served the landlords. The social and economic system of feudalism was inhuman and fragile, only to be overtaken by capitalism and technological revolution.

Industrial Societies: The 18th century witnessed a dramatic change as technological inventions paved their path faster than ever imagined. The industrial revolution introduced machines into our daily life, which impacted human social interactions rapidly in a short period. The invention of the steam engine by James Watt revolutionized the way humans worked together. The power of steam transformed the way textile industries worked. With new harvesting tools, agricultural harvest saw a new rise, and with gas lights, humans did get a night-life too.

Machines helped in building urban centers. Humans jostled together to work in the factories, thus creating new associations daily. The streamlining of human labor, power organization, and subordination soon became part of human interactions. Workers flocked to new locations causing a huge human migration towards the city, and there, sociology took birth as life was changing quickly and the long-established tradition of agricultural livelihood was diminishing. As humans faced newer environments, their behavior changed towards filth, poverty, and overcrowding, which opened a new perspective to studying human relationships. Consequently, exploiting daily workers increased, which led to radical changes in labor laws and human resource management.

Post-industrial societies: With the computerization and development of the internet, human social interactions have witnessed a magnanimous change. The present world encompasses digital societies where personal and professional connections develop with a click over a site. The evolution of emails made communications faster and more effective. Social networking sites like Facebook and LinkedIn have helped widen social networks. On the same note, human lives are now more inclined towards virtual interactions than face-to-face, which has a severe implication on the emotional quotient of the human mind. Society is now more divided based on technical skills, education, and information accrued. Post-industrial societies are information-based societies. However, using chemicals in food products in our daily life, acute diseases like cancer, blood pressure, diabetes, etc., increased in society.

Perspectives of Social Interaction

The functional aspect of society and social interactions in the modern world is filtered through three lenses.

Durkheim on Functionalism: Emile Durkheim stressed the interconnectivity of all the elements. He asserted that there is a clear distinction between individual behavior and collective behavior, as well as a collective conscience toward the shared values, ideas, and attitudes of society, based on the concept of social integration among different individuals. As per the functionalism perspective, a society works much like a human body, where every organ has something to contribute. As society evolved from the preindustrial to the industrial era, there was a shift from mechanical solidarity to organic solidarity. Society shifts towards more organic solidarity, and its development is halted. Social anomie became the new normal during this transition, where collective norms weakened.

Karl Marx on Conflict Theory: A society's economic structure forms the base on which the superstructure of culture and social institutions rests. According to Karl Marx, the economic structure of the society determines the characteristics, and the conflict in economic status is an essential contributor to change. Conflict and class antagonism have been consistent throughout the history of social reformation and human relationships in the social ambiance. William Blake's famous poem, 'Satanic Mills', is often considered the reflection of the exploitive attitude of the owners towards the working class. With the rise of industrialization and capitalism, human psychology altered. Modern human society is developed on the premise of alienation. The working class is isolated or divorced from society, work, and sense of self. Consider any working scenario of the present time. An employee is alienated from his own labor, the process involved, the product that is produced by his labor, and self-satisfaction. Humans are mechanized towards the wage received. False consciousness is developed in the process where the ideologies followed are never in the best interest of the human.

According to the conflict theory, humans connect with those belonging to the same social strata and try to improvise their condition. For example, a man working in the clerical division of an organization will not be comfortable mingling with the high-brows of the company. He will choose a society of his peers to live in. His children will go to schools that are affordable for his pocket. Developing a social relationship is aggressively connected with one's economic condition. And as the economic gap increases, the relationship is also crinkled.

Max Weber and Symbolic Interaction: This theory stands on the premise of rationalization. A society built with logic and efficiency, not morality and tradition, is called a rational society. Weber's interpretation of society reflects demarcation based on class, status, and power. While the economic condition determines class, religion, education, and kinship often contribute to status. And status and class, in turn, define the power of an individual.

The theory of symbolic interaction emphasizes the individual's viewpoint towards society and thus, impacts the way he/she relates to the social surrounding. The culmination of industrialization and rationalization evolution has trapped humans within institutions and bureaucracy. Human interactions have taken a giant leap in due course of time. For example, with more supermarkets and fewer family-owned stores, the social associations in the neighborhood have changed. With advanced cell phones and other gadgets, humans are happier while caged within the screen. Society's viewpoint has changed. A neighbor's concern is often mistaken as an intrusion. Technological development, digitization, and the advent of malls may sound rational towards making our lives easier. However, a staunch doubt hovers; are these universally desirable?

The Social Construction

The way human interactions help in building society is known as habitualization. This phenomenon depicts how any action repeated frequently becomes a pattern and how it is performed again in the future, in the same manner using the same economic effort. Society is more like a habit. Not only do we create this habit but also accept the way others have been performing. A society is built with consensus, both prior and current. There occurs a process of institutionalization to provide a convention and a norm. The moral codes and norms are defined with successive definitions of the situation. And humans interact based on the subjective construction of the norms and reality than the objective ones.

Language, gestures, and artefacts that people use to interact and interpret highly influence our interactive skills. In the social construction of reality, symbols play a crucial role in human communications and relationships. Similarly, our body language in the social ambiance reflects our values. For example, an introvert's body language is never inviting, thus limiting the human interaction at the beginning. Similarly, a verbose attracts more attention in public.

What Is Socialization?

Socialization is the process through which people are taught to be proficient and acceptable members of society. It is the sociological process that occurs through socializing. It involves how people comprehend societal norms and expectations, social beliefs, and values. In fact, physical tasks like sitting, eating, or talking are highly influenced by socializing. We, humans, are highly dependent on our social interactions to nourish our information and skills to be a part of society and also in the development of the self. Socialization is not only critical for children but also helpful in designing our ability to accept and adjust to a change.

Socialization is critical for the individual and the societies to sustain. It illustrates the complete intertwining of humans with their social world. A society perpetuates and sustains by teaching the norms to the new members. Social interactions serve as the means to make us able to see our worth through the eyes of others. And this, in turn, helps us to make ourselves fit for the world.

We are an outcome of the nurture we receive from our social relationships. Additionally, our nature decides on the nurture we receive.

Types of Social Associations

We learn many things from our social worlds that we cannot imagine in the beautiful world. There are several associations in the socialization process, from extended family to friends and peer groups. Families and extended peer groups teach us about the culture and the norms and design our first interaction with the tangible objects of the material culture.

I.

Extended Family

Socialization depends on teaching and learning about various things and concepts. The family is the primary socializing factor. The family is where the identification and learning of numerous objects, such as homes, neighborhoods, bicycles, public transportation, and other social life components, begin. Extended family members, such as grandparents, siblings, and cousins, are the first few to teach us the fundamentals of socialization, even if they are blood relatives and belong to the category of social relationships.

To understand the role of the family better, we must acknowledge that families do not socialize their children in a vacuum. A variety of social factors influence a child's upbringing. The attitudes toward socializing changed dramatically as society advanced. Six to seven decades ago, a father could publicly scold or beat the child to ensure discipline. In the current situation, openly reprimanding a youngster is regarded as verbal abuse. Psychologically, it is proven that a child's emotional growth is highly affected under such abusive conditions.

Additionally, a family's race, religion, economic condition, and educational background affect the socializing terms. For example, families with poor economic backgrounds show a strict upbringing. They emphasize conformity and obedience more than an economically sound family. Wealthy families emphasize nurturing creativity and judgments. Such influence is highly determined by the type of work the family does. Working-class parents perform repetitive tasks to earn their bread. They see the world differently and force their children to follow the norms. While economically sound parents mainly work in managerial positions where creativity and problem-solving form the basic course of work. They, in turn, wish to raise their children in the same kind of job environment. Thus, children are effectively raised and socialized to follow the type of jobs their parents are doing.

Children are socialized to abide by racial features and gender norms. Children perceive the social associations in a society where gender roles are equal. They grow up while behaving equally towards both genders. However, in a society like India, where patriarchy is the prevailing norm, children are raised to differentiate the treatment of men and women. A male child is raised to feel superior to the female child. The provision of higher education, freedom to choose a career, and decision-making role is bestowed more upon the male child.

In a conservative society like in Islamic countries, the interaction between two different genders is nearly prohibited. Women neither have many rights to education nor career growth. They are bound to the household chores. On the other hand, racial discrimination is nurtured as per familial values. In a country like the U.S., interracial couples are common in big cities like New York or Washington D.C. While one moves to the south of the U.S., a clear demarcation is observed. A child raised amidst an interracial ambiance understands the terms of equality more efficiently than a child raised in a more conservative mindset.

II.

Peer Group

People with the same age group, social status, and personal interests form a peer group in society. Socialization with peers starts in childhood, more prominently in the playgrounds. A child learns the basics of making friends and coordinating with each other and also understands the meaning of his/her role in the gathering. The concept of 'rules in life' is inculcated more profoundly through socialization with peer groups.

Peer groups form the first major socialization after families, although parents often influence the type of peer one nurtures. Let's assume a case scenario of affluent and economically weak parents to understand it better.

A scientist father would always like his children to play along with the children of his peers, who are equally affluent. Thus, the child would develop a knack for science, research, and technology during the growing years. On the other hand, a father who resides in a slum and earns through daily labor has hardly any opinion towards his child's friend circle. He might not know the difference between earning and stealing, all credit to the slum ambiance. The child will be inclined more towards that ambiance of the hardship. He will grow amidst people of different professions who are equally demeaning.

When a person develops his career goals, adolescence sees a higher impact on peer groups. A good company always ensures positive feedback towards our career choice. A teenager's goal is often influenced by the careers chosen by his friends. A career-focussed friend can inculcate the same inclination into a teenager who is otherwise wandering nowhere. A similar impact happens if the company is bad. Teenage crimes like eve-teasing, stealing, social vandalism, and sexual abuse are more often found to be an outcome of one's association with peers.

III.

Schools/Institutional Agents

Schools are not only a place to learn science, maths and other curricular subjects. School plays a vital role in our society because of good education and valuable lessons to the child's minds regarding knowledge, growth, and development. It provides knowledge to the child's mind and educates how a child interacts with different people in society. A child spends almost seven hours in school, learning some of the basic norms of life. Discipline, time management, taking down instruction, harmonizing with people around, respecting elderly people, and many more such learnings are a gift from the school. The classroom rituals of a teacher teaching help build the concept of role models. There prevails an informal curriculum within the schooling system, where one is taught about what the outer world expects from us.

For example, the school grading system helps the child understand where the child is lacking. On the same note, constant encouragement to perform well instills the feeling of competition. When children are given group projects, the main aim is to inculcate the habit of teamwork, division of labor, and coordination. Such disguised curriculum prepares the children for bureaucracy, rules, expectations, waiting for long hours, waiting for their turns. Schools also inculcate the concept of national pride, integrity, equality, and citizenship.

IV.

Neighbors and Neighborhood

Relationship with the neighbors is informal social relations that constitute a better part of our everyday life in contemporary urban societies. Sociological literature has an array of work demonstrating the benefits and adversaries of social connection with neighbors. The neighborhood studies were restricted to communities, initially.

There are fewer studies to analyze how neighborly relations are constructed and reproduced. However, research on gentrification has garnered more attention with pacing time. The most important aspect of neighborly relations is they refine our everyday mundane existence while answering several key questions of survival.

In a study conducted by Stokoe and Wallwork (2003), there is a remarkably very little definition of neighbors and experience in managing neighbor relations. Physical proximity represents the defining factor of neighbors. Being neighbors is entirely a different kind of relationship than being friends. The latter is consciously made; however, the former is what we get. The term neighbors have a spatial relationship. Considering the older definition by Heberle (1960), a neighborhood may or may not have physical boundaries or names. A long stretch of uneven road may act as a boundary between two distinct neighborhoods.

A neighborhood can view from an objective perspective of an observer and also from the subjective conceptions of the members. The objective definition reclines on the built and natural environment of the residential area with its physical boundaries and historical analysis of the residing community. The subjective perspective revolves around the ingrained culture, the extent of human interactions, mindset, etc. Sociologist Van Eijk (2011) concluded neighbors as those who live in the adjacent dwellings, next door, above, or below in an apartment system. Still, in a country like the U.S., independent houses are quite far from each other. In such cases, the neighborhood makes a sensible reference to a bounded geographical location. According to Abrams, a neighborhood is a defined territory or locality inhabited by people living in close harmony.

Knowing and socializing with neighbors provide a wide range of benefits, including enhanced safety and community events. A good neighborhood helps amplify happiness and combat challenges. Close and friendly relationships with neighbors help us create a meaningful life. A dynamic neighborhood encourages people to go out, mingle with others and have fun. This, in turn, ensures great emotional health with a sense of joy and security.

Maintaining a friendly demeanour with the neighbors helps share mutual chores and responsibilities. The neighborhood is the beginning of the initial friendship. Kids of similar age groups befriend each other, thus paving a path for the elders to interact. Neighbors are the primary eyes to watch over your properties. Our habits are inadvertently exposed to our neighbors; thus, they can detect any alterations from normalcy.

In the modern world, a neighborhood is the motley of language, culture, perspectives, and race. Therefore, growing up in an intercultural neighborhood always install the understanding of equality and democracy. As industrialization led to the migration of people, the dislocated souls always found a family in disguise amongst the neighbors.

Building a neighborhood community is the first step in crafting a harmonious surrounding. To be a good neighbor, we must initiate the relationship-building process in a positive mode. Gathering a few neighbors over a meal is always a good beginning. Always be generous, take the initiative and be participative. Encourage the new members to get involved and be resourceful. Distinctively, a good neighborhood grows through shared beliefs and ultimate desires. People harboring ulterior motives are never good for keeping harmony.

Neighborhood often constitutes the source of competition amongst the inhabitants. Parents compare their children's performances which in turn demoralizes the underperforming children. Similarly, children often compare their resources, which sometimes burden the parents financially. For example, every parent wants their children to be the best in curriculum. In this rush to make the child exceptionally well in academics, parents often overlook the other hidden talents in the child. On the same note, if one child in the neighborhood gets a new cricket bat or a new video game, every other child pesters their respective parents to get the same for them.

Social and symbolic boundaries like fences are applied to manage social distance and proximity between neighbors. These symbolic boundaries send out messages which cannot be pronounced verbally. The tone of voice, facial expressions, gestures, body language, and relation to doors and gates have a lot to reveal about the relationship between the neighbors. There prevails a difficulty in balancing proximity and distance in neighborly relations. A clear distinction is often missing to tag involvement as intrusion; i.e., the boundary between friendly supportiveness, interference violating privacy, or complete detachment is quite blurred. The friendly distance needs to be carefully worked out between the neighbors. Reciprocity is essential, however, not to the level of adversely affecting the private space.

V.

Religious Places

The human race has spent centuries trying to contemplate the meaning of life. This desire to comprehend the role and place of humans in the universe has nourished the role of God and religion. Since the evolution of human societies, religion has found its role in every society in some form or the other. Archaeological studies have revealed different kinds of ritualistic objects, burial ceremonies, and religious artifacts. The role of religion extended as staunch religious beliefs have been the reason behind several historical invasions and wars.

Religion has been integral in any social conflict.

Revolutionary socialist Karl Marx was one of the pioneers studying the social impact of religion. According to Marx, religion reflects the social stratification of society and remains the code for inequality, perpetuating an unjust status quo. Marx followers believe that religion is more like a false remedy for the economic sufferings of the working class. In his own words—religion is the opium of the people to forget all the injustice.

On the other hand, Durkheim analyzed the opposite; religion in terms of its societal impact. Religion binds people and brings social cohesion, promotes consistency in behavioral patterns, thus imposing social control. It also offers strength during life's transitions and tragedies. In applying natural science in the study of society, Durkheim concluded religion and morality as the collective mindset of society and that the cohesive bonds of social order result from common values in a society. These moral values should maintain to preserve social stability.

Political economist Max Weber stated religion was the precipitator of social change. He examined the effects of religion on economic activities. As a part of Protestant societies in the Netherlands, England, Scotland, and Germany were the most highly developed capitalist societies. The Protestant work ethic has a greater influence on the acceleration of capitalism. Protestant beliefs supported the pursuit of material gain by working hard and not spending on frivolous things.

Religion is a unified system of beliefs regarding sacred objects and moral practices. Religious beliefs and religious places form a crucial place to human interaction. Several studies have demonstrated that individuals more inclined towards religious practices carry better mental health. There prevails a salubrious effect of religion on human health. Potential theoretical perspectives reveal that involvement in religion benefits by developing a coping mechanism against stress. Religion, or precisely religious scriptures, somehow impart meaning to life, thus playing a vital role in alleviating the stress of wandering thoughts. Religious practices invariably inculcate better behavioral attitudes and help propagate healthier social interaction.

Religion is always associated with a place of worship, where people following the same religious beliefs gather together to follow the rituals. A country like India, which is the origin of Hinduism, is densely populated, with people following the Hindu religion. Temples have become commonplace in social interactions. Practices like religious feasts and festivities, funerals, meditations and initiations, sacrifices or services, cultural fests, etc., bring a good platform for social interactions. Many new relationships are built on the threshold of temples, mosques, churches, and other religious places. In fact, arranged marriages are often fixed in such places. Not only personal relationships but also several business prospects grow through religious rituals.

Social scientists recognize religion as an organized and integrated set of beliefs, behaviors, and norms centered on basic social needs and values. Religion is a cultural universal found in all social groups and helps build social relationships. Religion supplies differing degrees of social cement that hold societies and cultures together. Faith justifies society's existence beyond the mundane and partial explanations of existence through science. Faith gives an impetus to action.

Religious faith nurtures our intention to create harmonious human bonding.

VI.

Work Places

An employee spends an average of 8 hours a day at the workplace. A healthy ambiance and symbiotic work relations are crucial for the organization and employees. It is essential to feel connected, appreciated, and supported by colleagues, subordinates, and superiors. Work relationships positively and negatively impact employees' minds, creating stress and reducing productivity and general well-being of their life. The psychosocial hazards due to the organizational culture, such as poor interpersonal relations and a lack of policies and practices towards ensuring the basic emotional needs of employees, are the major cause of work stress. Prolonged exposure to these psychosocial hazards is related to increased psychiatric and physiological health problems, and positive social relationships among the employees can soothe the issue.

When work and family responsibilities collide, all should make a balance between them. For example, most male employees neglect their families to succeed in life by focussing more time on work. In turn, they lose their family relation after a certain year due to absence from social function in their families. The children suffer most because they feel bad when one parent's absent from school functions. Hence, we must strike a balance between work and family. Focus on kids' education and wishes, and spend valuable time with your love, especially on weekends. It is possible with mutual understanding and co-operation.

Much like neighbors, colleagues are not friends with respect to bond formation. We don't make colleagues, and we get them as they are. Optimistic and encouraging colleagues are a boon to any workplace ambiance. The social relationship among the employees plays a vital role in deciding whether the organization will flounder or flourish. A bad working environment is the first cause of attrition.

Decade-long psychological studies of workplaces have identified the desire to feel connected to others as a basic human need, with interpersonal relationships significantly impacting mental and physical health, behavioral patterns, and even mortality rate. Human physiology is profoundly affected by positive social interactions. Gable & Gosnell (2011) observed that humans could separate reflexive brain networks for social thinking. Close and comfortable relationships are linked to the production of happy hormones that fight against the adverse effects of stress. The neurotransmitter oxytocin is released in response to social contact, which in turn helps in developing the emotion of trust and motivation. On the other hand, Dunbar and Dunbar (1998) have concluded that emotional pain, as received through social isolation and public humiliation, is quite equivalent to physical pain.

Additionally, cooperation, trust, and fairness at the workplace activate the brain's reward center and encourage future interactions. It promotes employee trust, respect, and confidence, with employees believing the best in each other and inspiring each other in their performance. A physiological study by Heaphy & Dutton (2008) showed that positive social interactions strengthen physiological resourcefulness by improving the cardiovascular, immune, and neuroendocrine systems. Cardiovascular reactivity is reduced, and metabolic disorders are controlled with good social connections at work. In short, when employees experience positive relationships, the body is more capable of building, maintaining, and repairing itself both in the workplace and also during non-work-related leisure and resting times.

Organizations with higher levels of employee engagement carry lower business costs, improved performance outcomes, lower staff turnover and absenteeism, and fewer safety incidents. Social interaction leads to knowledge and productivity transfer from the trained to the untrained workers, in collaborative team settings or between senior and junior workers, in case of low-skilled tasks and occupations. An organizational study conducted by Mas and Moretti (2009) proved that productivity improved when employees were assigned to work with a more knowledgeable co-worker. Business leaders who encourage informal interactions, like social gatherings outside official hours, foster more positive relationships, and significantly influence and improve employee satisfaction.

Strong ties developed by social interactions nourish inspiration and sponsorship and pave for innovation. Social interactions bring all the employees on the same page towards organizational goals. These peer relationships exist between co-workers with no formal authority over one another and act as an important source of informational and emotional support for employees. Co-workers with knowledge and experience of their specific workplace experience are given opportunities to feel connected and included by sharing information through regular social interactions. Social interactions in the workplace have been found to increase self-reported positive feelings at the end of the workday (Nolan & Küpers, 2009). When trust exists between team members, they are more likely to engage in positive and cooperative behavior, increasing employee access to valuable resources.

Negative ties between two individuals at work are characterized by animosity, exclusion, avoidance, and lack of reciprocity and are independent predictors of medically diagnosed depression. Employees tend to be involved in many dyadic relationships within the workplace, with individuals generally possessing both negative and positive ties. However, when individuals have more negative associations with co-workers than positive, they often face adverse outcomes such as social ostracism.

Social interactions at work have indirect effects on personal relationships. A good human resource policy ensures that colleagues help the new entrants at work in finding accommodation and other familial matters. Colleagues often guide in finding good schools and other extra-curricular activities. Social interactions with colleagues help bridge the gap in pursuit of personal relationships.

Conclusion

Social relationships are interspersed in every other form of relationship. A personal relationship between a man and a woman initiates through socializing. Socio-political influence, business relationships and organizational ethics serve as the extended branch of social relationships. A study on social relationships is an entire domain in itself.

CHAPTER SEVEN

ROLE OF SOCIAL MEDIA IN HUMAN LIFE

Social media is like crack-immediately gratifying and hugely addictive.

— Gary Vaynerchuk

Introduction

Since the advent of human communication, media and technology have been interwoven in developing our social associations. The printing press, newsrooms, internet, and social networking channels have paved a peculiar yet interesting web of social communication. While growing up, humans develop connections in the real world; however, in the recent decade, virtual connections have become an integral part of our social life for individuals and associations. There has been a steady decline in the number of people meeting up over coffee, either at home, at a shop, or hanging out for a movie. In fact, with the rising use of social media, humans are more prone to declare even our illness to the whole world through a tweet, Instagram, WhatsApp, or Facebook post. There is a dramatic shift in the way social connections are made and interact with each other. Technology has changed the mere part of speech of the word 'friend.' More than a noun, a friend is more like a verb that is involved in the action.

An internet-based technology that facilitates sharing ideas, thoughts, and information by building virtual networks and communities is broadly defined as social media. It gives users quick electronic communication of content, and news, including personal information, documents, videos, and photos. Users engage with social media through a computer or a smartphone via web-based software or applications. Social media is omnipresent now, and countries like Indonesia lead the list in social media usage. More than 3.8 billion people are registered on some other social media platform.

Social media has changed our perspectives. We are more outspoken in the virtual world, question the ongoing government policies, raise our voices against social and political injustice, and share information at lightning speed. However, has technology changed our social perspectives for the better? Posting about the ice-bucket challenge, copying and pasting a post about cancer awareness, or propagating a hashtag topic on our social media handle. Does this reflect our true intent, or are we just running the rat race? There is a constant and immediate flow of information, to such an extent that social scientists have concluded this as a source of distraction in the guise of entertainment. This, in turn, often makes the working class complacent with the social inequities.

There are several issues to watch when viewed through the lens of sociology. A functionalist focusses on the social purposes of technology and media. For example, the internet serves as a technology and media, and it links individuals and nations in a communication network that facilitates small family discussions and global trade networks. A functionalist view the manifest functions of media and technology and their contribution to social dysfunction. On the other hand, the conflict perspective focuses on the systematic inequality created by differential access to media and technology. For example, how can a working-class individual be sure that the news they hear is not morphed for political interests? Similarly, the interactionists will ponder upon the difference between the real objective of the world and the scenes showcased in reality shows.

There is an array of sociological imaginations where the impact of media and technology on society and social interactions is studied.

Technological Intervention in Daily Life

From the steam engine to robotic surgery tools, humanity has come a long way, holding the hands of science and technology. Today, as we sit before our laptops and swipe through our iPhones, we might wonder about their abilities to solve human problems. However, the truth is that the present technology may be obsolete in the next few decades.

While most people see only computers and cell phones as an outcome of technology, we must acknowledge that technology is not merely a product of the modern era. All our technological inventions are like advancements of the previous iteration. For example, fire and stone tools were important forms that technology during the Stone Age. Much like the beneficial effects of digitalization in the present world, the creation of stone tools changed how pre-modern humans lived and gathered food. From the first calculator, invented in 2400 BCE. in Babylon in the form of the abacus, to the predecessor of the modern computer, created by Charles Babbage in 1882, every innovation has been built on the premise of easing human life. And indeed, all aspects of our lives today are influenced by technology. The introduction of machines in the field of agriculture has drastically reduced the need for manual labor and set only a few rural jobs. This, in turn, led to the urbanization of society and also lowered the birth rates, considering the fewer helping hands required. Similarly, the advent of DNA fingerprinting has dramatically changed the scenario of criminal justice.

It is well known sociological fact that not everyone is bestowed with equal access to improvements in human society. Greater innovations resulted in larger knowledge gaps. And based on the technological stratification, this gap gets wider faster. In short, the gap gets wider faster.

There are two types of technological stratification. The first is called the digital divide, i.e., the differential class-based access to technology. It leads to a knowledge gap, which is the increasing information gap for those with less access to technology. Simply put, students in affluent schools receive more exposure to technology than students in poorly funded schools. Those students with more exposure gain more proficiency and become more acceptable in an increasingly technology-based job market. This divides society into those with technological knowledge and those without. This widening gap has serious implications while initiating social interactions. Someone lacking computer knowledge in the 21st century will be hesitant to start communicating with people working with computers. The digital divide often leads to an inferiority complex. A study on the digital divide by Guillén and Suárez (2005) states that this global digital divide is contributed by both the economic and socio-political characteristics of the country. As far as social associations are concerned, people basking in the same technological stratum associate together.

Use of Social Media

It is a common question in everybody's mind what is the psychological impact of social media on our minds? How often do we use the cell phone? How to control the use of your cell phone?

Global statistics have revealed that when it comes to cell phones, 67% of the users check on their phones for messages or calls even when the phone isn't ringing. In addition, 78% of cell phone owners sleep with their phone next to their bed to avoid missing any calls, text messages, or other updates on social media during the night. In the present scenario, 100% of the cell phone users describe their cell phone as something they can't imagine living without.

While the cell phone has made it easier to stay in touch, simplified planning and scheduling their daily activities, and increased their productivity, it severely impacts our attention span. We are very often distracted. We cling to a single notification on our social media page for a minimum of five minutes to scroll up and down to gather more information.

The major question is, how do we get to know we are addicted to our cell phones? We use our cell phones most of the time and are unable to cut back due to the habit of boredom, feel touch with fiancé, and greetings of friends. If we do so and are out of cell phones for an hour at that time, we feel depression and anxiety in our minds, and fear of losing our relationships comes into mind. We all feel that adolescents' mental and physical health is associated with cell phone addiction. On the other hand, the young generation's screen-based working culture and lack of physical activities rapidly increase the eye problem.

Present-day parenting is adversely affected as children hardly get attention from their internet-addict parents. Behavioral scientists have found that 73 % of adults are engaged in some social networking online. The most widely used platform is Facebook, and members of both Facebook and Instagram platforms often visit their websites. One-third of the users check their social media pages more than five times daily. If we check our Facebook friend list, we can introspect how our virtual social connections are far more than our real-world connections. The significant question that keeps cropping up is about the trustworthiness of such social connections. However, social media has become a powerful agent in bringing societal change. No matter where one is on earth, one can get acquainted with anybody from oceans apart. Social media has imparted a voice to the voiceless. Initiatives over the global economic crisis, climate change, gender equality, and LGBTQ rights have been represented more profoundly than ever imagined on the global platform.

It isn't easy to conceive of any one theory to explain the variety of ways in which people socialize and interact through technology and media. Technology runs the gamut from the match you strike to light a candle all the way up to sophisticated nuclear power plants that possibly power the factory where that candle is made. Media could refer to the television we watch, the ads wrapping the bus we take to work or school, or the magazines we shuffle through in a hospital's waiting room. Along with comes Instagram, Facebook, Blogs, YouTube, etc. However, are media and technology critical to the forward march of humanity? Or are they pernicious capitalist tools that lead to the exploitation of workers worldwide?

Social networking is a phenomenon that has existed since society began. Two human beings have always sought to live in social environments. The proliferation of social networking sites and their pervasion in everyday practices affect how societies manage their social networks. To a significant extent, the social association has shifted from social networking to the internet. In less than five years, these sites have grown from a niche online activity into a phenomenon through which tens of millions of internet users are connected, both in their leisure time and at work.

In the present scenario, users are willing to embrace social media sites as a means of communication and social networking in everyday life. The increasing dependence on technology for basic communication also highlights the importance of analyzing how social media affect daily life and work. Sites like Facebook, Friendster, and LinkedIn also influence how users establish, maintain, and cultivate social relationships, from close friendships to casual acquaintances to professional connections. Various factors led to the consideration of the implications of these technologies for policy-making.

With the growing use of social networking sites, students' academic performance showed a steep decline. Teenagers are found to be addicted to various gaming sites and pornographic obsession. The level of distraction in the working class is so profound that many offices have locked the social networking sites through their internet service.

Concern over Online Privacy

We have indeed increased our digital footprint by going online to connect socially, share material, conduct business, or store information, which has increased our vulnerability to those who are surfing the web with criminal intent. With the rising number of cybercrimes, more than 60% of internet users are concerned about their online privacy. In a survey conducted in 2018, 43% of global participants indicated that they had been harassed online, and 17% indicated that many of their personal information, bank details, and online transactions were hacked.

Online privacy and security are key organizational concerns as well. The large-scale data breaches during 2013 at retailers such as target, financial powerhouses such as JP Morgan, and cell phone providers such as Verizon, exposed millions of people to the threat of identity theft when hackers got access to personal information by compromising website security.

Cyberbullying

Social interactions are never free from bullying. Be it in school or college, one experiences some bullying, either from seniors or teachers or even classmates. However, with social networking sites, bullying over the web is gathering attention from a socio-psychological perspective.

Cyberbullying is bullying done over digital devices like cell phones, computers, and tablets. It can occur through text messages, Facebook messenger, WhatsApp, other social media platforms, dating apps, online gaming stores, and any online portal where people can view, participate in, or share content. Cyberbullying mainly includes sending, posting, or sharing negative, harmful, false, or mean content about someone to humiliate in public or blackmail in return for monetary favors. Cyberbullying is a criminal offence and has become a big blotch over social media-based socialization. Cybercrime is increasing daily due to fast communication through mobile and laptops/desktops. The objective of crime is hacking, phishing, and spamming. Cybercrime also induces child pornography and blackmailing the victim of sexual activities. We may call it a computer crime.

There are top five cybercrimes affecting businesses and individuals are as under:

- Phishing scams
- Website spoofing
- Ransomware
- Malware
- Internet of things (IoT) hacking

With the prevalence of social media and digital forums, our comments, personal photos, viewpoints, and shared content are available in the public domain and can be easily viewed by strangers and acquaintances; whatever individual content is shared creates a kind of permanent public record of their views, activities, and behavior. This public record is more like an online reputation, which is accessible to schools, employers, colleges, clubs, and others, whoever wants to know about the individual. Cyberbullying can harm the online reputations of everyone involved – not just the person being bullied but those doing the bullying or participating in it.

The major concerns about cyberbullying are:

Persistence – Social media never sleeps. Once logged on the internet, any information, true or false, will be available globally, almost immediately.

Permanent – If not reported and removed, most information communicated electronically is permanent and public. A negative online reputation, including for those who bully, can impact college admissions, employment, and other areas of life.

Psychological impact – Victims of cyberbullying are prone to depression and often refrain from socializing.

Effects of Social Media on Relationships

Social media is the newest and most accepted mode to connect. It has several good and bad consequences on every form of relationship; whether romantic or platonic or professional. On social media, we connect with people who not only share our interests but also our anxiety, misery, fear, and celebrations. About 83% of teens globally, feel secure and comfortable in initiating interpersonal relationships on social media platforms. These platforms have become the new hub for fostering romantic relationships, especially for the marginalized sections like LGBTQ+ communities who have lesser options in the real world. More than 55% of LGBTQ+ members are involved in dating online. People challenged with social anxiety, geographical isolation, insecurities and another myriad of socio-psychological issues have found solace in this kind of virtual connection.

Keeping aside the beneficial aspects of social media in building social connections, it has some negative implications on human relationships.

- **Unrealistic Expectations:** Over the years, it has become 'cool' to profess one's relationship status on social media handles. Different couples have different economic statuses, however, while scrolling down on others' magnificent posts, a sense of competition often crops up. Couples try to match their life with others through some unrealistic expectations. The problem isn't restricted to only romantic relationships. Sibling relationships, social associations with friends and colleagues also get affected.

- **Cause of Envy:** Sense of comparison often kindles envy. The achievements posted on social media hardly motivate anyone these days. One's better days lead to an envious association with the other.

- **Fake:** Social media is propagating fakeness, if not anything else. Every kind of relationship is veiled under a façade of all-good. Celebrities fake their beauty, relationship status, lifestyle, further instigating new and unrealistic desires amongst the commoners.

- **Open Privacy:** The present world is busier in showing off than any action. People are adamant about buttressing their associations, whether business or personal. Private lives trade on social media handles for the sake of marketing. Celebrities breaking up in the public, posting videos of domestic violence are some of the new fads.

- **Opining is a Trend:** Whether one has enough knowledge on a topic or not, one is eligible and also technically free to opine anything on anyone or any topic. For example, people far from the reality of Afghan situations post their opinion on how India should have performed.

- **Disruptive:** The trending posts, viral videos are quite addictive. Don't we keep scrolling down our phones before sleeping? Bedtime stories are the days bygone. Bedroom intimacies have become more of a job to produce children. Social media has disrupted the natural flow of emotional and relational needs.

Positive Effects of Social Media

a) Social media helps people meet each other:

In our digital area, it's not uncommon for people to meet online or through dating apps. It may be more common. A 2017 survey found that 39% of heterosexual couples reported meeting their partner online, compared to just 22% in 2009. A later study analyzing the results found that internet meeting displaces the roles that family and friends once played in bringing couples together. According to a recent Tinder survey, online dating can be especially helpful for the LGBTQ+ community. Of 1,000 LGBTQ+ adults who took the survey, 80% say online dating and dating apps have helped their community, 52% feel more comfortable being themselves, and 45% say exploring their identity is easier.

b) It can keep you connected to your partner:

According to a survey published in the *Cyberpsychology, Behavior, and Social Networking journal*, young adults in long-distance romantic relationships can better maintain them using social networking sites. Whether sending a funny meme over Instagram or taking a quick Snapchat, social media is easy for couples and family members to interact throughout the day in a fun, low-pressure manner. This is particularly helpful for couples who don't live together and people in long-distance relationships. People who have their partner in their profile photo or relationship status on Facebook also tend to be happier with their relationship, for what that's worth.

c) You can learn about relationships from experts:

There are plenty of accounts that offer up good information to help develop and maintain a healthy connection. Relationship bloggers and psychotherapists, provide counseling online through their social media pages.

As long as the relationship comes from a place of growth and not a comparison, this type of social media can motivate you to work on parts of the relationship that have been neglected earlier.

d) A time capsule of memories:

Social media platforms have practically replaced printed photograph albums as a place to store and share memories. In this sense, an individual can use social media platforms to honor her/his activities and the things you create together. Unlike a physical photo album, social media has the added component of followers. In this way, social media can be an institutionalized way to express love publicly and invite community support, both of which enhance social relationships to flourish.

Has social media become more valued now?

Social media platforms are designed to snare our attention, keep us online, and have us repeatedly check our screens for updates. It's how the companies make money. But, like a gambling compulsion or an addiction to nicotine, alcohol, or drugs, social media use can create psychological cravings. When you receive a like, a share, or a favorable reaction to a post, it can trigger the release of dopamine in the brain, the same chemical that follows winning a competition, taking a bite of chocolate, or lighting up a cigarette. The more we are rewarded, the more time we want to spend on social media, even if it becomes detrimental to other aspects of our life.

Conclusion

In our fast-paced life, we cannot deny the usefulness of social media in enhancing our social connectivity and business relationships. As every technological revolution has come up with pros and cons, social media has played a significant role in influencing human relationships. Although social media has helped build wider social and business networks, it has inflicted much bitterness on the essence of human relationships. Social relationships lay bare on the walls of social media channels, prone to intrusion, bullying, and emotional torture. Written communication is cryptic, and poor communication skill alters the meaning of what is actually intended. The common human emotions of jealousy, competition, comparison, and boastful attitude have come out of latency in this present generation of social media addiction. Similarly, addiction to social media is drawing much attention, and there are counseling programs to detox oneself from social media addiction.

CHAPTER EIGHT

Economic & Political Relationships

One of the penalties for refusing to participate in politics is that one ends up being governed by one's own inferiors.

— Plato

Introduction

The word 'Politics' is derived from the Greek word Politika, meaning affairs of the city. Over the years, many historians have attributed their own unique derivative definition to this term. However, the general consensus is that it can contemporarily be defined as the set of activities that are associated with making decisions in/for groups, forming power relations with individuals or forming relationships for the distribution of resources or status. Many scholars have devoted their time to studying this branch of social science that deals exclusively with politics and the government, and a new terminology was assigned to it, referring to it as Political Science.

Politics, as an entity, is best understood through understanding the science behind it. Political Science helps us understand exactly the aim of politics and how did it come about to influence human society as we know it today. Postmodernism political science is generally divided into three main disciplines of Comparative Politics, International Relations, and Theory of Politics, with the former two assuming greater significance in today's globalized economic conditions. Within this, there are further notable subdivisions such as Public Policy and Administration, Domestic Policy and Government, Political Economy and Political Methodology.

Historians and scholars have broadly termed Political Science as the social study which analyzes the allocation and transfer of power in decision making, roles and systems of governance, political behaviour, and public policies. Through Political Science, an individual can measure the success of governments and the implementation of specific policies through the examination of various factors viz. stability, social justice, material wealth distribution, the prevalence of peaceful conditions, and health of the public. These specific factors have been a part of each historian's record over the years and thus have been made as a barometer of analysis when considering a political study of a local governing body. To know how these arose, it befits us to understand a bit more of the history and evolution of Politics as a Science.

Origins and evolution of Politics and Political Science

The precursors of western politics can be traced to the Greek Socratic era of philosophy, though certain historians differ in their conclusions. Aristotle is widely regarded as the first to give a working definition of Political Science around the year 335 B.C.E. He is said to have stated that Political Science is a branch of science powerful enough to eclipse other branches of science since it concerns the governance of the common masses. Plato took it further by placing significant emphasis on the scientific aspect of Political Science. The Roman historians such as Livy and Plutarch also echoed this line of thought and concurrently documented not only the rise of the Roman Empire but also the rise and fall of other nations and how the Roman Empire maintained relations with those nations. Livy, Plutarch and another noted historian Polybius recorded that leaders such as Julius Caesar and Cicero implemented policies of their own will in order to centralize their power base. Caesar, in particular, was noted to have implemented strict policies to keep the general public in line; however, he also implemented certain reforms that would ultimately end up benefiting the people (one such policy was granting Roman citizenship to external immigrants or the downtrodden for them to avail benefits of the Roman Empire). Plutarch also notes that during this time, Political Science was more about understanding the impact of governing bodies and how rulers enforced laws. Over the thousand-year period of the Roman Empire, various political leaders saw fit to impose their own laws (mostly on a whim or in some cases through external pressure) and Polybius notes that this hardly affected the Institution, which was considered as the backbone.

In India, the predecessors of ancient politics lie in the four holy Vedic scriptures. As was with the western civilization, during the 3rd-century BCE, Chanakya wrote the Arthashastra, a political treatise that discussed international relations (with different empires of the time), war strategies, and fiscal policies. One of the most notable aspects of Arthashastra was that it espoused a system of equality amongst the masses, but at the same time equated work and opportunities for individuals based on their talents. Chandragupta Maurya, Chanakya's protégé, made good use of this treatise to build upon the Mauryan Empire in India and was regarded widely by historians as the most benevolent of kings. His reign was characterized by a booming economy, brimming state coffers, general happiness amongst the kingdom's populace, and respect amongst his peers. The Mauryan Empire would become a foundation upon which the concept of Aryavarta or present-day India would be built.

As the saying goes, times change and so do people. And so did the concept of politics and political science with the passage of time. The fall of the Roman Empire led to a period of uncertainty in Western Europe and this period is commonly referred to as the Medieval Age or the Middle Ages. A more diffuse political arena arose as a result of new kingdoms, which then led to varied political beliefs and tenets. A monotheistic society brought a new light to the political arena and political action. This is exemplified in the works of Augustine Hippo's The City of God, which synthesized current philosophies and political traditions with those of the beliefs of Christianity. Borders were redefined between what constituted as being political and what was religious. In India, the Mauryan Empire had fallen and its fractured feudatories now had virtual dominance amongst their serfs. Manusmriti was produced, which formed an important political treatise for governing a disparate populace at a time of unrest, more on the basis of a person's origins and work rather than their economic status.

During the Renaissance period (12th Century to 16th Century), Niccolo Machiavelli emphasized modern political science through direct observations of political institutions and actors. One notable observation of his was that even evil means needed to be considered in order to acquire and maintain a ruler's state for establishing governance over the populace (leading to another well-known terminology – Machiavellian scheme of things). Similarly, Thomas Hobbes' Social Contract Theory stated that a strong power like the monarchy was imperative to govern the selfishness of an individual but there must be no divine right bestowed upon the monarchy. The Renaissance led to a new set of political rules and empires and nations brought about new norms which went against the established conditions.

As time passed, the Enlightenment Era (17th to 18th Century) saw the works of French philosophers Voltaire, Diderot, and Rousseau presenting the political analysis, social science, critique of society, and polity. The French Revolution to topple the monarchy and subsequent establishment of modern democracy in Mainland Europe is mainly attributed to their works. Most noteworthy of this period was that the state was separated from all religious activities, which led to a more effective political discourse being undertaken. A new nation in the form of the United States of America saw its founding fathers Thomas Jefferson and Benjamin Franklin also making their contributions to political discourse.

The onset of the 19th Century AD saw the rise of the Darwinian models of evolution and natural selection. Well established political policies saw a marked upswing in the development of countries but general living conditions of humans were still slow to improve. The Industrial Revolution saw the most tumultuous phase of human development and political science played its part. Industrial output took precedence over consideration for human life. Often, workers were forced to toil in inhuman conditions, yet no one complained since work meant to pay for the meal at the end of the day. Life expectancy, which was on the rise in the 19th century, suddenly plummeted due to widespread diseases and a rise in air pollution. World over, the governments and their policies were more oriented towards rampant expansion and the quest to find more resources for filling up the state coffers. In the pursuit of this, if a few people (or nations for that matter) fell by the wayside, it did not matter much to the people in the high chair. This ruthless expansionist mentality of the old colonial powers eventually led to two global cataclysmic conflicts which would eventually shape society as we know of today.

Policies affecting Global Economy

The advent of the 20th century heralded a neo-dark age for the world in terms of politics and political science. As stated before, the 19th century was more about the European Colonial powers establishing themselves at the head of the table for bragging rights (resources for their main country). Their policies in their respective colonies would eventually spill over to Mainland Europe to cause a global catastrophe in the form of World War I. The colonial powers of Germany, the Austro-Hungarian Empire, the Balkan Kingdoms, the

Ottoman Empire, the French Republic, the Russian Empire, the USA, and the British Empire, all jostled for securing resources to further their ambitious plans. What resulted was a 5-year long war of attrition dubbed 'The War to End All Wars'. Around 10 million combat casualties and close to 25 million civilian casualties occurred which set the world back by about 20 man-years. The Macro and Micro effects of World War I was felt. Families were devoid of men who were killed in combat, throwing women into the formal workforce for the first time in history. It also led to the suffrage movement for women in many countries, gaining women voting rights and greater economic independence. World War I's economic policies also led to the advancement in technology in many of the great powers. USA and Britain became pioneers in aviation due to their scientific superiority. Germany's Ruhr Valley and the industries in Essen became a gold standard in steel manufacturing and a lot of the other countries adopted these techniques to further their own industries. These technological developments were further refined down the years.

However, not all was well in Europe. The victors of the First World War had carved the continent in their imagination, leading to the festering of hatred in many of the nations who had lost the war; notably in Germany's Weimar Republic, which had ceded the lands of Alsace, Lorraine, Sudetenland and parts of northern Baltic coasts. This led to the rise of the Nazi Party in Germany led by the fanatic Adolf Hitler, who spewed anti-Semitism in his speeches, as well as giving the clarion call for regaining the lost territories which 'rightfully belonged to Germany'. In the Far East, the Imperial Japanese Army led by the tyrannical General Tojo began making incursions into Manchuria, the Philippines and the Pacific

Islands. Inevitable skirmishes followed and another full-blown world war, commonly known as World War II plagued the world from 1939 to 1945. A total of 80 million casualties were recorded with the civilian population bearing the brunt of it due to the rampaging invading forces. All this stemmed from one man's policies, rhetoric, and fanaticism, along with another Imperial power's conquest for its resource-starved nation. The economic policies established during World War II had more repercussions than those established in World War I. For example, Britain was still a formidable power with far-flung colonies and it extracted every ounce of blood, sweat and tears from its colonial vassal states of India, Burma, Indochina and Malaya. Men were thrown into the war, resources used for funding Britain's war effort and food from the colonies was transported to the British mainland. This led to starvation amongst the local populace and festered general discontent. Famines became regular and mass civilian deaths were reported as a result. One such disastrous economic policy by Winston Churchill's War Cabinet led to the Bengal Famine in India, causing the death of close to 2.1 million people from starvation alone. Another 1.5 million people died as a result of the spread of diseases like Malaria, Typhoid and Cholera. Around 2 million people were also displaced due to loss of livelihood and agricultural lands turning barren. These incidents, coupled with the general hatred of people against British rule led to India gaining independence in the year 1947.

With the end of World War II, a governing body of all nations was setup to prevent future global catastrophes. The United Nations came into existence in the year 1945 with many branches under its ambit. One such branch is the International

Monetary Fund (IMF). Also set up in 1945, its primary task was to help the member states to cope up with the financial crisis that plagued the end of World War II. Leading economists from all different countries came together to set up a system of rules for the IMF to monitor the economies of countries, help in capacity building and lend money when and where required; all to promote stability and economic growth.

The IMF's presence has played a key part in the organization of the international economic system by overcoming political differences in its member states. The design of the IMF has allowed the economic system to balance the rebuilding of international capitalism along with the maximization of national economic sovereignty and human welfare; a concept also known as embedded liberalism. The influence of the IMF grew steadily with the rise in the number of members states of the UN (and by default the IMF). As many countries in Africa attained political independence, and the Soviet Satellite States broke away from the Soviet Union after its dissolution in 1991, the IMF became a more powerful entity and global policies became easier to enact. The IMF's policies have uniformly benefited the member states without being partial to any one particular economy. However, criticism has always been there from the newer members, who state that the IMF's role has been relegated to more of being a mouthpiece for the P5 group (USA, UK, France, Russia, and the People's Republic of China) of the UN.

Political Diplomacy

Diplomacy plays a key role in maintaining political relationships between two different countries. When the two states in question have similar political beliefs, the more harmonious is the diplomacy between them. More often than not, the two states in question have differing political beliefs, often leading to moments fraught with the danger of escalating into a crisis. Political stability between two countries is a matter of avoiding economic and financial crisis, swings in economic activity, inflation, volatility in foreign exchange, and unstable financial markets. The challenge for policymakers and diplomats lie in minimizing instability in their own country and abroad without reducing their country's economy's ability to improve living standards through rising productivity, employment, and sustainable growth. Therefore, political diplomacy plays a very important role in today's interconnected global economy. Modern diplomacy largely originates from 17th Century Europe and slowly became professionalized in the 20th Century. In 1961, the Vienna Convention on Diplomatic Relations was ratified by most nations, thereby providing a framework of diplomatic procedures, methods and conduct of diplomats.

Some of the earliest known political diplomacy records are from the peace treaties signed between two warring Mesopotamian City-States of Lagash and Umma in 2100 BCE. The ancient Greeks often dispatched Proxenos to negotiate specific issues such as war, peace, or commercial relations with foreign sovereign states. Political diplomacy in the older eras was often achieved by marrying a woman of the opposing side to strengthen a political alliance. Alexander of Macedon was recorded to have married a Sogdian woman, Roxana, from the Bactrian Kingdom, in order to placate the rebelling local populations. Similarly, Chandragupta Maurya of the Mauryan Empire in India married Helena, the daughter of the Greek General Seleucus Nicator to put an end to the hostilities and extend his empire.

Modern Diplomacy was first recorded when the State of Milan sent representatives to the court of the French King in 1455 but refused to host representatives from France suspecting espionage. Soon, the tradition spread across major European powers and each of them had a representative in the other power's country. In this period, the rules of modern diplomacy were furthered and refined. The word representative was changed to 'Ambassador', derived from French which was the most dominant continental language in Europe of the time. The concept of Diplomatic Immunity took shape and standards were set on how to treat these Ambassadors and how the Ambassadors must behave in other states. Slowly, Eastern Europe and Russia also adopted these standards. However, diplomacy took a hit during the time of the French Revolution and the rise of Napoleon Bonaparte. He arrested and imprisoned many British officials under the suspicion of scheming against the French Republic and refused to accord Diplomatic Immunity to anyone.

In due course of time, following events of the two World Wars, the International Court of Justice (ICJ) was established as a major arm of the UN to settle arbitrations in a diplomatic manner. One famous example is the formation of the Hay-Herbert Treaty which was brought to the ICJ by the diplomats of the UK and the USA to settle disputes at the international border between Mainland USA and Canada. Sometimes, arbitrations of the ICJ are not acceptable by the diplomats of the two states in question and an independent third party is called to act upon as a mediator. Accords are signed between the two states. One such example is the Camp David Accords signed between Israel and Egypt for a peace treaty, mediated by President Jimmy Carter of the USA. Weeks of negotiation among President Carter, Prime Minister Begin of Israel and President Anwar Sadat led to the signing of the Accords, leading the Israel-Egypt Peace treaty of 1979.

There are different types of political diplomacy practised over the years. Appeasement Diplomacy is often considered a failure since the appeasement of colonial powers was what led to the two World Wars. Hostage Diplomacy has been practised ever since the evolution of civilization and as the name suggests, involves taking hostages to win a political battle. One recent example is the hijacking of Indian Airlines Flight IC814 by terrorists to secure the release of their brethren lodged in Indian Jails. Quiet Diplomacy, or Preventive Diplomacy, involves the use of covert methods to gain political one-upmanship. A recent development is a Debt-Trap Diplomacy where countries with huge political and financial powers lend money to a debt-ridden state at low interests, thereby saddling the borrowing country with huge debt till it reaches the state of signing over the country's assets to the lending country.

The People's Republic of China has been accused of practising this in Africa and South Asia. Scientific Diplomacy is the use of scientific collaborations to advance the political interests of one country in another. A few notable examples are the building of the International Space Station, CERN Laboratory and the recent Vaccine Diplomacy practised by India during the COVID-19 crisis. Finally, there is Soft Power Diplomacy where a major country's culturally attractive factors pre-dispose people of a foreign culture to sympathize with them. The most noted example is that of Hollywood movies and Bollywood movies having the soft power to charm the audiences in foreign countries, thereby creating a favorable impression of the USA and India in those countries viewing those movies.

Impact of currency devaluations and change of interest rate on the economy:

Rising inflationary pressure across the globe, continuous Foreign Institutional Investors (FII) selling, and the rupee depreciating to an all-time low has turned investors' sentiments negative towards the capital market.

Geopolitical tensions arising from Russia's invasion of Ukraine have resulted rising in commodity prices across the globe and put pressure on the domestic currency. The cost of all imported materials has gone up. Subsequently, the corporate margin decreased due to increased raw material or import costs. On the other hand, the corporate will enhance the product's price to maintain the profit ratio. Inflation will go up due to a rise in product prices; as a result, the country's growth will hamper, and unemployment will increase.

We may call it a multi-level cause-and-effect relationship due to currency devaluations.

The durable consumer companies are, in fact, battling a trifecta of problems: high commodity cost, Covid-induced lockdowns in China, and a depreciating Indian Rupee. It will further push up the import cost and shrink the margin. On the other hand, the cost of working capital increases because of the rising interest rates, which also induces them to increase the product prices. Ultimately, we, the general public, pay the higher prices of the same product due to currency devaluation and supply-demand mismatch.

During the persistent depreciation of the rupee against the US$, the small exporter will be adversely affected due to volatility and further currency weakness. Any strength of the Rupee vis-à-vis Dollar, the forward contract made by the exporter will lose. However, the small exporter is unable to sustain this loss. Although a weaker currency bodes well for exports, that does not apply to all the export units.

What type of relationship is it? Every action is related to good and bad cause and effect; one should understand it. You have to understand the economy in line with the Government and the Central Bank (RBI) policies. The rising interest rate by the Central bank constrained the economic growth, which has caused for recession and adverse effects in the long run on all economic parameters. People of Sri Lanka suffer a lot due to the non-availability of food grains, only due to the Government's ban on all chemical fertilizers in 2021, resulting in drastically cutting crop production in the country.

The growth engine of India Inc. is mainly affected by four factors:

- Rising Crude prices & sky-high Inflation
- Devaluation of the Indian Rupee due to the stronger US Dollar
- Rising interest rates adversely affect industrial growth
- Sudden fallen of foreign exchange reserves

Hence, external (Macro) and internal (Micro) economic factors, in conjunction with political turmoil, affect India's growth.

Impact of Religion on Political Relationship

The relationship between religion and politics continues to be a tenuous theme in political science, despite numerous charters calling for the existence of clear conscience in individual thinking and separation of religion from the State. It is well known that religions often make stronger claims on people's allegiance, and universal religions tend to claim all these people rather than favoring just one community. Most commonly seen in Islam, the religion believes that all people owe allegiance to Allah, the Supreme God, and must bend to His will. These religious commitments have inevitably led to a conflict in the political arena, where most political parties and states are perceived as Liberal and Atheistic. But it is also seen that religious beliefs ultimately end up supporting politics and political decisions in some way or the other. Though religious minorities in different political spheres are due for their share, it ends up being appeased based on religion rather than ethnicity, gender, or economic condition. It proves a fertile breeding ground for dissatisfaction amongst many religious groups.

In the wake of the Protestant Reformation in the Western Hemisphere, the European Societies wrestled with determining the Church's role and what that of the State was. The democratic governing body of the Church would reject the influence of the Church and remain atheistic. Still, it would allow leaders to be religious since cutting themselves off from tradition and convention completely, religion would also be devoid of the State of ethical wisdom and would lead to tyranny and social/cultural fragmentation. So the seeds were sown to keep a part of religion in the State.

Contemporary liberals appeal to the typical value of 'fairness.' In their opinion, a state should remain neutral towards any form of religion, especially a democratic government, since it is supposed to represent all the people comprising its demographic. However, liberal tradition abhors the intrusion of religion into the Government in any form or manner. Slowly, as society became more pluralistic in terms of religion, one of the paramount problems was whether and to what extent religions needed to be tolerated from a political viewpoint.

John Locke, in his treatise A Letter Concerning Toleration, notes that

a) it is futile to attempt and coerce the belief of an individual since it does not bend to a will,

b) it is wrong to restrict religious practice so long as it does not interfere with the rights of the others and

c) allowing a wide range of religious groups is more likely to prevent the rise of one majority group to preserve the general peace in the populace.

Nevertheless, religious fault lines have pervaded the current political system. The rise of religious, political parties was observed after the Second World War, the most famous example being the formation of Israel and the disintegration of the Indian sub-continent into Hindu Majority India and Muslim Majority Pakistan. Especially in the latter two, the problems persist even today. Though the problems in India and Pakistan have been mostly attributed due to the diplomatic decision of the British Empire, it is undeniable that religious fervor and rise in the religious-political divide much before the British left contributed a major factor to the Partition of India.

Religion also plays a major role in shaping a country's internal political system. Take the example of the People's Republic of China. The Communist Party of China (CCP), in its manifesto, proudly states that the country is a Pluralistic Society, with each individual free to partake in a religion of one's own choice. However, closer scrutiny reveals that the CCP, fearing their loss of power during the nascent stages of the country's formation, favored the atheistic Han populace, thereby leading to a new revolution. Religions were abhorred, either voluntarily or coercively. The majority of the population in today's China is atheistic. Peering into the looking glass, one can see the scars of the Uyghurs in North-western China, Tibet on the borders with India, and the Inner Mongolia region bordering Mongolia. Crushing of dissent, reorganizing political beliefs of the local populace, and modifying their language were carried out on a large scale that the local population there knew scarcely more than the history of Han Chinese, spoke no further than Mandarin, and ate no more than Han Chinese delicacies.

Personal perspectives affecting political relationships

When the term 'intergovernmental' is used in any context, it is always underscored by political undertones. In a multicultural world and a globalized economy, the working relationship between two states must be free from any caveats. However, history has shown us that this is not always the case. There are numerous examples where the relationship between two countries is fraught with tension due to various political squabbles. The two most prominent examples are the relationship between Israel and the Islamic Middle Eastern States and the relationship between India and Pakistan.

The relationship between Israel and the Islamic Middle East is tenuous. Israel follows a policy of non-appeasement and no negotiations regarding terrorism. The higher officials and the powerbrokers believed that the Land of Judea rightfully belonged to them, and they were forcefully evicted during the various skirmishes in the distant past. So when the Western powers carved up the land of Palestine into three parts, Israel gleefully accepted what was handed to them on a silver platter and ruled its dominion with an iron fist approach to external elements. One can see these effects as Israel has become a technological pioneer and is renowned for turning vast tracts of barren land into the most fertile of places while maintaining a no-nonsense approach to any kind of threat to stability.

The Middle Eastern Islamic states of Egypt, Lebanon, Syria, Jordan, and Palestine protested that the land belonged to Palestine and was the holy birthplace of Islam. Israel, on its part, was more than accommodating to carve up the eastern borders willingly, but the Palestinian Liberation Organization wanted nothing less than the total disbanding of Israel. Hence, the PLO often resorted to underhanded activities, which provoked an iron-fisted response. Hundreds of thousands have perished in an unnecessary power struggle that could have been avoided only if the political establishment of either side were willing to compromise. All it would have taken is a bit of diplomacy and tact to solve a thorn in the Middle East. Instead, it has become a tinderbox waiting to explode at the slightest provocation from either side.

On the other hand, India and Pakistan have a lot more in common. People speak similar languages, eat similar food, and can find their intertwined history on both sides of the border. Mohini Hameed, Pakistan's first lady radio news anchor, better known as Shamim Apa, was born in Batala in Punjab, India. Manmohan Singh, former Prime Minister of India, was born in Gah, Pakistan. L. K. Advani is an Indian politician who served as the 7th Deputy Prime Minister and is one of the co-founders of the BJP; a senior veteran politician was born in a Hindu business family in Karachi, Pakistan.

Despite all this, the political turmoil between the two countries can be solely attributed to the pervasive religiousness in the political hierarchy of Pakistan. Dilip Kumar was an Indian actor and film producer with ancestral roots in current Pakistan and Muhammed Ali Jinnah's father was born in Kathiawar in Gujarat. India has made numerous attempts to be a big brother despite all the past antecedents, while Pakistan plays truant only due to its politics being controlled in the name of religion.

Every overture by India has been met with stiff resistance and religion may be a cause.

What makes it even more dangerous is that the nation is a nuclear-armed state and the religious zealots sit on a veritable stockpile of nuclear weapons enough to destroy the entire Indian Subcontinent.

Conclusion

Politics comes with a preceding factor of effective leadership. From our inception as social animals, we humans chose to follow certain rules and restrictions of our society. We grew as a community by first choosing a leader who could guide us to lead a better life. A leader who could solve the existing problems became the most influential person in the community. The present Government, under the leadership of Hon'ble Prime Minister Shri Narendra Modi, tries to maintain a good relationship and resolve countries' issues worldwide and work on the principle of "Vasudhaiva Kutumbakam" and ideals of "Sabka Saath, SabkaVikas, Sabka Vishwas, Sabka Prayaas" to build an Aatmanirbhar Bharat. And his perspectives towards life shaped others' mindset. As human psychological studies have revealed, humans are inherently followers, and we constantly seek guidance at home, work, or in life. To seek guidance, we interact and develop bonds with other humans. Social interactions are no longer restricted to the mere neighborhood. We develop global human relationships these days. The political relationship is built through the country's vision and mission, along with the emotional quotient of the political leaders. Thus, cultural background, education, religious beliefs, and political outlook do influence human equations with each other. Two countries that are politically inclined towards the same goal have their respective citizens living harmoniously with each other.

Similarly, outrageous differences in political outlook often instigate emotional outbursts and distort human relationships. Humans are highly influenced by the residing country's political pressures and their relationships with others. Culture, religion, and politics are the three most influential elements in shaping human behavior and communication skills and, in turn, impact human relationships. Political relationships between countries are key factors in shaping human's conception of the other country's citizens and, in turn, craft their ability or inability to develop compatible relationships.

CHAPTER NINE

WHAT RELATIONSHIP DO YOU HAVE WITH YOUR COLLEAGUES?

Is it okay to be friends with your colleagues? Like them or loathe them, we cannot escape the people we work with. We, as working adults, spend around one-third of our day at work, and much of this time interacting with colleagues either directly or virtually. Further, our colleagues can become key players in our social life through romantic liaisons or bridge organizational boundaries. Our colleagues provide us with social support and advice, but they can also be a source of negative behaviors such as bullying. Thus, while we may seek to establish relationships with our colleagues, these work relationships will vary greatly in how and why they develop and in the outcomes they produce.

Employees will form strong bonds with other colleagues,

some enjoyable and mutually beneficial, while with other colleagues, they may form more neutral or even negative relationships and try to avoid interactions as much as possible. Human resource is one of the essential ingredients of any organizationand working in a conducive ambience with positive human interaction always enhances performance. A high-performing team is formed only by good and strong human relationships.

A common saying in the corporate world is that Colleagues can never be friends. However, over the years, many organizations have made sure to maintain a healthy atmosphere at the workplace. Flattened hierarchy in the organizational job profile has a tremendous effect on developing harmonious social relationships.

Romantic Relationship at Work

Online surveys and academic research over the last few decades have clearly illustrated the prevalence of workplace romance; it has been suggested that workplace romance has been on the rise over the last 50 years. Workplaces are now recognized to have an important sexual activity. Still, the pervasive nature of romantic and sexual relationships that prosper at work is rarely discussed in the literature. Workplace romances are defined as mutually desired relationships involving sexual attraction between two employees of the same organization. Romantic behavior is well distinguished from sexually harassing unwelcome behavior. Workplace romance is supposed to be a consensual relationship between two employees of the opposite sex that does not constitute unwanted or harassing activity. The bookish definition has excluded the involvement of heterosexual partners. There has been an ongoing notion that the influx of women in the workplace has increased the rate of workplace romance. In fact, workplace romance has been a cause of increased divorce rates, too, across India.

Attraction at work tends to happen between those who work in close proximity, collaborate together to accomplish their work, are similar in attitude to each other, and find it easy to interact. Working together fosters an increase in the interaction among co-workers as well as a sense of common purpose and goals, which increases the likelihood of personal attraction. Sharing a subjective experience, such as a similar reaction to another person or event can also lead to interpersonal attraction. A substantial proportion of the research literature shows that job productivity can be negatively affected due to romantic activities: excessive chatting on social media platforms, long lunches and extended discussions behind closed doors, missed meetings, late arrivals, early departures, and costly errors. Other negative effects include co-worker disapproval, cynicism, hostility, and concerns about whether there will be favoritism and employment benefits given to one person in the relationship by the other.

Organizational Politics and Human Relationships

People often regulate their emotions, suppression, and expression, to ensure desired outcomes in a relationship or adhere to accepted situational norms; however, the overall intensity of felt emotion is rooted in the strength of the relationship. Emotions that are deemed beneficial to the relationship, even if not necessarily positive ones, like anger towards a common enemy, and remorse over a mistake, enhance perceptions of relationship value. While those deemed detrimental to the relationship reduce that value. More detailed expectations than weak relationships often characterize stronger relationships, and expectation confirmation and disconfirmation are major drivers of emotional reactions in relationships. Communication, expectations, perceived responsiveness, and emotions are shaped by partners' ability to understand one another in a given social context. Work relationships include interactions between two employees that accomplish common objectives and goals within an organizational context, making them unique.

Many work relationships are derived from an organization's formal hierarchy or organizational structure, meaning that partners must interact with one another to achieve work-related goals such as favorable performance evaluations, promotions, and so forth, whether they choose their partners or not. Political skill is essential to achieve favorable outcomes in these relationships. Those who possess political skills can accurately assess their work environments, understand others' motives, and recognize the impact of their own behavior. This allows them to more effectively influence others through the use of political behavior that is appropriate for the dyadic partner and the relational context.

It is important to view work relationships as different from familial or social friendship relationships. Work relationships tend to revolve around social influence, and those who are more politically diplomatic form better relationships at work. Being inherently constrained and permeated by work-related goals and systems, work relationships necessarily involve social influence behavior; recognizing this fact helps reduce the stigma of organizational politics and may let people more effectively interact with one another and meet mutual goals. Enacting political behavior can benefit not only oneself but also one's organization. Practitioners can benefit by encouraging people to influence one another to meet benevolent goals that satisfy self, partner, and organization, and in doing so, may create a more dynamic and adaptable organization.

Gender Roles in Workplace Relationships

The interplay of gender and relationships in any context is complex. Gender is a person variable (females and males differ) and a stimulus variable (females and males are perceived and treated differently). The composition of the workplace plays a major role. Women and men will find socio-emotional support and friendships more easily in settings where their own gender is in the majority. It is also possible that women seek and expect emotional support from their relationships at work more than men do. The relatively higher status of men in most work settings also creates a different context for men and women seeking to build hard social capital. Whereas men can do this in a homophilous network, women must cross the gender line to network with powerful men.

Work is a place in which complex and meaningful relationships occur, both positive and negative, both lateral and hierarchical, but in every case, these relationships are also gendered. Whether the relationship is same-sex or cross-sex, whether the power differential favors the man or the woman, or whether the relationship is mostly work-related or personal, gender will contribute to how individuals act and react. Gender will affect how others perceive the individuals in the relationship. Because relationships in the workplace also affect how individuals perceive the job itself and how satisfied, committed, and productive they are, gender and relationships in the workplace should be an ongoing focus of research in industrial/organizational psychology.

Bullying at Work

Many employers and employees recognize or should recognize that physical assault and ritual humiliations are unacceptable at work and maybe break the law. But what about the verbal assault, such as telling someone they are worthless? Bullying at work can severely affect targets' health and well-being, causing self-doubt, anxiety, post-traumatic stress symptoms, and depression. The most harmful forms of bullying are those that lead targets to lose their sense of self-worth and to feel excluded, such as unfair criticism, undermining, hints they should quit, being ignored, and having their private life criticized. Physical health can also be affected, including an increased risk of cardiovascular disease. These effects can last five years or more.

Conclusion

For organizations, positive relationships between colleagues prove beneficial. They may attract employees in the first place and can support employees to act more supportively and collegially. Friendships' impact on an individual's work experiences can be profound, improving satisfaction and commitment, increasing cohesion, and reducing intentions to leave. Yet relationships may not always progress as we might hope. We may not establish the good working relationship with our manager that we want, or we may find that a particular colleague is persistently petty and undermining. Workplace bullying can affect individual employees leading to absenteeism, depression, and even suicide. Clearly, there are serious risks to bad workplace relationships. The globalization of work also makes it important to develop productive relationships with colleagues from different cultures. Proactive behavior is defined as being self-starting, change-oriented, and future-focused. It is imperative to examine how relationships can influence perceptions of proactive behavior.

CHAPTER TEN

BUSINESS RELATIONSHIPS

The business of business is relationships; the business of life is human connections.

— Robin S. Sharma

Do you think a successful business is all about closing down a sale? As Patricia Fripp, the famous executive coach, once quoted, a successful enterprise is built through building and maintaining long-term relationships. While running a business, nothing is more important than working on building a conducive working ambience and effective human relationships. Human interactions happen at various stages and in various forms, thus forming different types of business relationships.

A simple outline would predict the following business relationships.

- **Employee Relationship:** Any business begins with the human resource in the organization. Better the workforce, the better the productivity. Sir Richard Branson has often quoted, 'If you look after your staff, your staff will look after your customers'. As stated in the previous chapter, a conducive working environment helps employees develop better relationships at work, and thus they become a high-performing team for the organization.

- **Customer Relationship:** Clients and customers are the souls of any business. Every business is online in today's market and stands bare on the global platform for public scrutiny. No organization can prosper in the market without building a strong and trustworthy relationship with its customers. Any bad feedback over a company and its products on an online portal can ruin the company's name. On the other hand, the organization's online presence and technological advancement provide the best business relationship with the client/customers.

- **Mentors and Peers:** Effective leadership drives the workforce to reach the organizational goal, and similarly, good bonding between peers develops social capital in any organization. Mentors and peers help at every stage of one's career right from the induction and are significant in both workplace relationships and business relationships.

- **Competitor Relationship:** Every business has one of those competitors that keep it on its toes. They are innovative, creative, active, and honestly a thorough pain. One would never seem to be able to keep up with the competitor, and they always seem to be flying ahead of the game. Similarly, every blooming business has certain things that the competitors always admire. Instead of feeling threatened by their skills, befriend your competitor and work out a deal where one could work together with their competitor. Sound relationships with competitors can benefit the overall society with joint efforts.

- **Legal Relationship:** To sustain any business in a country, one must know the rules and regulations of that country and the legality that prevails for day-to-day business. For example, the marijuana business is legal in the Netherlands, but the same cannot be legal in India. Every country has a constitutional law to follow, and every business runs through maintaining legal relationships with the country's judiciary system. As they say in the legal world, one must be honest with his lawyers, no matter how big the crime has been. Lawyers know their way out; if a business wants to crack any deal, it must have its legal advisor team in confidence.

- **Financial Relationship:** The finance section is the backbone of an organization. A sound financial relationship of an entity shows the growth of that organization. Hence, Accountants, Financial Advisors, and Banking Officials are crucial for any business growth. Without having strong bonds in the finance section, other sections may not be able to deliver good results to the organization. The Finance Head also examines the organization's inner workings, gets a prudent decision on all financial proposals, and also analyses what's really going on. They are the ones to declare your business viable or not. Finance people make or break you. You may find that the advice given is not the best without good people in your corner. This, in turn, could see one making some decisions that do not serve one well. So, a business must ensure that whoever one gives this level of trust is worthy of it.

- **Stakeholders and Corporations:** Working with other corporations and stakeholders creates value in business relationships. A good and sustainable relationship comes with strong collaborations and good business ethics. These provide added value to the company and build some extra strong relationships that could serve us for years to come based on the sustainable business practice in their operation. Companies with greater transparency in their system, actions, and practices create good business relationships with stakeholders and corporations.

Ways to Build Business Relationships

Like a personal relationship, business relationships require continual follow-up with clients, corporate, companies, and stakeholders.

A mutual benefit and ongoing communication are important ingredients to success and maintaining a business relationship. In the long run, having close and trusting contacts will give an edge, especially when other marketing tactics fail to work.

- **Reach Out to Important Contacts**

Having weekly or monthly conversations with every contact in the CRM system is impossible. But one can focus on the valuable ones. Pinpoint the best clients, partners, and vendors and continually check upon them. Express interest in their business. If you want to keep the relationship alive, make this outreach routine. If you let too much time go by, your eventual contact will seem less genuine. And don't ignore the power of your LinkedIn connections. When executed properly, a social media strategy is the digital sister to in-person networking – and it can be a fast and efficient way to ensure you are routinely reaching out.

- **Offer Help Before You Ask for Help**

Building business relationships doesn't mean tapping into your resources whenever you need something. If you ever contact a former client only when you have a new service offering, your gesture won't seem authentic. Similarly, don't expect to get one if you call your vendor only when you are looking for a good deal.

- **Ask for Feedback**

Instead of assuming your clients and vendors are happy, ASK OUT! Open communication is the basic component of any relationship. When you ask your contacts how they feel, you promote a two-way conversation that can uncover areas for improvement. Some firms conduct client satisfaction surveys to gather feedback.

- **Educate, Don't Sell.**

If building relationships requires trust and credibility, then educating – as opposed to selling – is a big enabler of professional services relationships. If a business relationship is not working, the individuals and companies involved should try to dissolve the relationship without creating further damage. They should address the issue head-on, explain what is not working and suggest a reasonable course for the parties to extract themselves from the relationship. Knowing how to resolve these issues properly can differentiate between an unsatisfied customer and a PR nightmare. For the sake of the company's reputation, never rush out of a bad client relationship without coming up with a viable compromise.

Impact of Stress on Human Relations

Have you ever been to a day when you reach home tired from work and suddenly realize that you've forgotten to send an important mail to one of your clients? You rush to open your laptop all over again and realize how you lack time for yourself. As soon as you open your mail, you find another job assigned to you by your supervisor. You have a promotion impending; thus, you try to work on the assigned project beyond your working hours to impress your boss. You work relentlessly for a month and produce expected results; however, the desired promotion goes to your colleague as the management used a different guideline to measure performance.

How do you feel? Do you feel cheated? The colleague who got the promotion is a very close friend and has helped you in difficult times. But now, as human psychology takes center stage, you develop a kind of bitterness towards this colleague. As the colleague is a woman, your mind plays a different trick by bringing her gender into the foul play. In a couple of days, you forget all her goodness, disregard her meritocracy and start considering her as the biggest villain of your life. Your mind chalks out an entirely different storyline for your career. You decide to shirk your job, but do not take any mental rest as you are too busy to nurture a crippled mentality for a mere promotion.

Now, is this scenario new? Never! This kind of deterioration in human relationships is often found while studying business relationships. And considering the psychological studies, stress has been found to play a major role in damaging human relations. Over the years, technology has greatly improved our work culture. Every worker is connected, and the projects are completed swiftly. On the same note, it has increased the level of competition to an unhealthy level and, in turn, has resulted in work stress. Hans Selye defined stress as the body's nonspecific response to a demand for a change. Change is inevitable, and it takes time for a human mind to accept and adjust to the change. There are different kinds of stress which are reproduced below:

- **Acute Stress:** Normally comes from demands and pressures of the past and future. As per the above example, you have been stressed about getting the promotion and avoided quality time with your friends and family. It battered your relationship with your spouse, children, and other family members.

- **Episodic Acute Stress:** You are always stressed as you think you have worked hard, but management didn't recognize your efforts. You are stressed because you don't think about anything beyond your work. You have become a recluse as your colleague has been given something that you wanted. In the whole process, you have lost touch not only with your family but also with your colleagues.

- **Chronic Stress:** As you fail to nurture healthy relationships at home and work, your work ethic has changed. Colleagues are less helpful towards your efforts, and you fall prey to chronic stress without realizing that your human relationship skills have gone for a toss.

- **Eustress:** This is also known as positive stress. Imagine that a female colleague of yours has now become your boss, and instead of highlighting your reclusive mannerisms, she chooses to bestow you with some valuable responsibilities. She picks out your hidden talent and lets you set a different and better goal altogether. You get a positive thrust to work better if you find no bossy attitude in your female colleague.

Stress often influences our ability to manage conflict at work. Stress can shut down our ability to think rationally and feel emotions. When stress occurs, shutting down our emotions doesn't allow us to make rational decisions, nor does it allow us to be emotionally available to others. Stress can affect our ability to communicate and work effectively with people at work. People who are stressed often are impatient, poor listeners, and may lose their sense of humor. These temporary behaviors that occur when stressed can impact how others see us and how well we interact with them.

Communication in Business Relationship

Communication is the essential ingredient of preserving human relations as it is the only means we have of expressing ourselves to others. In other words, every relationship we have built has relied on communication for it to be successful. Those relationships that may have been unsuccessful could have resulted from not understanding each other's communication styles. No? How often have we heard our colleagues tell us there's been a miscommunication? It is a common phenomenon in business as any piece of news travels from one desk to another and gets edited; either content is added to the actual information or deleted.

Communication relates to relationship management and social awareness skills, which are part of emotional intelligence. These skills allow us to communicate with others and handle various personalities and work styles. The first step to applying communication skills is first to understand your style. Are you direct or indirect? Do you know how facial expressions and other nonverbal language impact your verbal communication? When you write an e-mail, how does your communication style come across to others? Understanding our style can help us understand our strengths and weaknesses and become better communicators. And effective communication is essential to creating and maintaining a harmonious business relationship.

Inclusion of Diversity at Work

Diversity at work refers to the inclusion of human resources from different cultural, linguistic, social, and racial backgrounds. Humans are inherently keen observers. Given a chance to explore something new, we often work beyond our expectations. Inculcating an inclusive work culture certainly helps in building better business relationships. The present world works on the function of GLOCALIZATION, i.e., think globally and act locally. Tamilian planning to open a South-Indian restaurant in Paris must develop cordial relationships with the locals. Similarly, a French perfume company cannot garner profits in India from day 1. Over the years, globalization of businesses has happened on the strong foundation of sound business relationships.

A diverse workforce enhances our quality of work life. Diverse work culture is a source of cultural enhancement and helps develop better human relationships worldwide. For example, a Nigerian colleague won't have anything to celebrate for Diwali; however, his Indian colleagues can make him feel their own by including him in their festivities. Multiculturalism goes deeper than diversity by focusing on inclusiveness, understanding, and respect, and also by looking at unequal power in society. Businesses can attain greater profitability through a diverse work environment and multicultural understanding.

Success in working in diverse environments comes from using emotional intelligence skills such as relationship management and social awareness. These skills allow us to understand how another person feels or why they do something, even if we do not agree. These skills also allow us to be accepting of others and appreciate differences even though we may not like them. Developing the skills to work in a multicultural environment can help us work with people from any variety of backgrounds and also helps us to communicate better with everyone we may come across, both professionally and personally. These abilities, acceptance, and understanding are cornerstones to developing positive relationships that lead to positive human relations and work success.

Conclusion

The way of doing business has evolved to a new stage where Return on Relationship is more significant than Return on Investments. Businesses today concentrate more on building and maintaining effective relationships with employees, customers, stakeholders, shareholders, and even the governing bodies. Effective communication is the key to having a successful business relationship. Always remember, your business is run effectively only if your employees reach their personal goals along with your organizational goals. And secondly, customers are indeed God in today's ever-changing marketplace. A customer retained is another customer gained. A symbiotic relationship with the competitors can open better avenues for the business. As humans form the basic structure of any organization, better human relationships pave a concrete path towards success.

CHAPTER ELEVEN

Managing Stress in Relationships

"When I look back on all these worries, I remember the story of the old man who said on his deathbed that he had had a lot of trouble in his life, most of which had never happened."
—Winston Churchill

The connoisseur of English Literature would think of Shakespeare's Hamlet when anyone talks about stress in human relationships. 'For who would bear the whips and scorns of time!' amlet has put the most suitable words in the melange of human relationships. Two humans participate in building a bond; however, as time changes its tone, humans too unmask their true colors to concentrate only on their personal needs. Two humans, no matter how much they love each other and how strong their bond is, are still two different entities who are looking at life through a different lens. Some minds are myopic, while others like to roam freely, unchained by rules. This difference in ideologies slowly grows and cultivates stressors in every relationship over time.

We thoroughly understood the different kinds of human relationships in chapter 10. As we know, no single relationship is devoid of conflict. Be it mother and child, married couples, colleagues, or political parties on global platforms. The prerequisite of stress is CHANGE. Incorporating a new lifestyle, accepting a partner in life or business, adjusting to the growing needs of teenage children, and shuffling through political turmoil in the country and everything around is bound to produce physical and emotional stress. However, does that mean a man can abandon all his bonds and become an island? No. People come in all shapes and sizes, and so does the relationship difficulty. Some of it is very minor and temporary, as the effects of small events as bad moods, poorly chosen words, or inept actions. While some of it feels less transitory in nature and importance, more endemic and more typical of the person in whose presence it is experienced. In short, some difficulty is attributed to people to people.

If we ever imagined that relationships are all smoothness and joy and that the difficulties of relationships can be bracketed off to one side, then we have utterly misunderstood the nature of the relationship. Everyday life confronts us with many tensions and difficulties in relationships which are entirely common and natural elements of the whole process. Whether we are dealing with difficult neighbors, having power struggles at work, dealing with abusive in-laws, the problems of handling long-distance relationships, the regrettable consequences of a hook-up, gossip, enemies, the dark side of relationships, stalkers, violence, or just those irritating little buggers who make life difficult from time to time, we relate everything as stressful relationships. However, while pondering on the negative sides of the relationships, it is important to recognize that some minor but inherently distressing routine rubs necessarily balance the delight which is felt in the company of the loved ones.

These can unexpectedly involve us in obligations to perform duties for partners or to carry out favors that may cause us personal inconvenience. Still, we compromise on certain aspects in the workplace and at home.

That's how human relationships are. They have good and bad stuff in them, even the best and strongest relationships. The experience of everyday life relationships is surely one where challenges are managed against balancing positivity or rewards. For the most part, we do not notice the management that we do day-to-day in our ongoing relationships because we know that that is how the cookie crumbles, and we are not dumb enough to expect everything to go well all the time. On the same note, managing stress is important to brew healthy human relationships as the elders would say: one should know when to shut up.

Understanding Stress in Relationships

Dealing with relationship stress is never easy; still, it's part of life. Even if your partner has consistently been the anchor in your relationship, eventually, there comes a time when their strength is trembling, and you will be asked to provide love and support. And while you may find it to be difficult to help your partner during times of stress, generating the mental and emotional resources to help your partner will create comfort and connection and a healthy, secure base in the relationship that both partners can consistently count on. When people are stressed, they become distracted, withdrawn, and less affectionate. Leisure activities are consigned to the back burner, which creates alienation from social groups and family. Stress brings out our worst traits. We're depleted of cognitive resources, which makes us hyper-vigilant and oversensitive to criticism. Since we're more irritable, we're more likely to fight over issues we'd normally drop – and if relationship stress were already a problem, it would increase tenfold when external stressors are added to the equation.

Hectic schedules and everyday work-life demands make it easy to become wrapped up in our own worlds. But when we lose sight of the stress our partner, parents, or children are going through, then we are not communicating enough, and we are losing the connection. This is why it is imperative to make the extra effort to recognize when dealing with a stressed partner.

Do Gender and Age Play A Role?

The human mind acts and reacts differently at different stages of life. Children and aged people are more vulnerable and fragile emotionally and are more adversely affected than adults. Teenage comes up with two divergent reactions where different stressors impact teenagers differently. Some would take the stress as a challenge and shape a new future altogether, while some may get negatively influenced and end up with mental issues, drug abuse, etc.

A similar study has been found in the case of genders. Though women are not considered as strong as men; however, their emotional tenacity is found to be more adjusting. Men and women react differently to stress. One of the fundamental reasons for this is the varying stress hormones. When stress strikes, the body releases cortisol and epinephrine hormones that raise blood pressure and circulate blood sugar levels. Oxytocin is then released from the brain, countering the impact of cortisol and epinephrine by relaxing emotions. This, in turn, instigates several emotional stressors.

Men release less oxytocin than women when they are stressed, meaning they have a stronger reaction from both cortisol and epinephrine. A study published in Psychological Review suggested that this caused women to be more likely to handle stress by 'tending and befriending' – nurturing those around them to protect themselves and their loved ones. Men, however, release smaller doses of oxytocin, which makes them more likely to have the 'fight or flight' response when it comes to stress, either repressing their emotions and escaping the situation or fighting back.

Impact of Stress on Health

Now, when there is such a hue and cry over managing stress in human relationships, it becomes indispensable to chart out the major side effects of stress. Whether we talk about stress between parents and children or colleagues, human physiology doesn't distinguish between the relationship kinds when responding to stress. Relationship stress can lead to mental health problems like:

- Anxiety when you are around your partner/child/colleague or the person responsible for your stress.

- Overanalyses of your interactions
- Inability to control your emotions
- Depression
- Sleeping difficulty

One study even showed that in ambivalent relationships where interactions turn hostile, physical health also starts showing significant changes like;

- Stomach issues
- Skin problems
- Increased risk of heart disease
- High blood pressure
- Weaker immune system

How to get rid of these health issues?

You can manage your health issues in two ways: changing your dietary pattern for daily routine and practicing regular yoga. For the former, you have to consult a dieticianor physician, and for the latter, you follow the instruction of a Yoga Guru.

Sources of Stress

Learning how to manage this stress is one of the first steps in ensuring we are mentally prepared to nurture our relationships at work and home. But, before even trying to manage stress, we must find out the cause of our stress. We can divide these stressors into personal stresses and work stresses. Although we divide them for ease, it is intuitive that if someone is experiencing personal stress, he or she will also experience it at work, resulting in lessened workplace performance.

A) Work Stress: Some of the common causes of workplace stress include the following:

- Long hours and increased demands: Due to increased technology, employees are expected to be available to answer e-mail on weekends and evenings. As a result of this added work time, employees find less time to engage in leisure and household activities such as grocery shopping and cleaning.
- Being treated unfairly: It includes bullying and being overlooked for promotions and appraisals.
- Lack of control: Too much supervision is unhealthy for the boss-employee relationship.
- Lack of job security office politics like favoritism and conflicts.

B) Personal Stress: Every relationship is interconnected. Our personal life influences our productivity at the office and vice versa.

- Daily Challenges: Even a leaking water heater at home can stress you at work.

- Personality: Impatient, aggressive characteristics lead to more stress in relationships.
- Work-life balance: Anything too much is not good for any relationship. Too indulged in work snatches your time with family and thus induces stress in a personal relationship.
- Financial hurdles: No one wants to be deprived of the luxuries of life. An overzealous attitude often leads to stress.
- Friends and Family Issues: As social beings, our lives are highly influenced by our surroundings. An ailing family member or loss of friendship is a significant personal stressor.

Thus, before you start managing your stressed relationship, you must endeavor to find out your stressor. Every ailment has a medicine of its own.

How to Reduce Stress in Relationships?

We all experience stress at one time or another. However, we can take action to assess and relieve the stress in our life. First, we do some self-analysis to determine the stressors in our life and how we handle them. This emotional intelligence skill allows us to see what we need to improve upon. Then, we can apply self-management tools to help us manage the stress in our lives. The benefit of this identification and management is that it allows us to relate better to others both in our work life and personal life.

Psychoanalytic has provided four steps to manage and reduce stress.

1. Avoid the stressor. We can try to avoid situations that stress us out.

2. Alter the stressor. Another option in dealing with stress is to try to alter it if you can't avoid it. When changing a situation, you can be more assertive, manage time better, and communicate your own needs and wants better. For example, if you find your opinions are disturbing your teenage child, try to understand his point of view.

3. Adapt to the stressor. The best way to move on with life is to accept, adjust, and accommodate.

4. Accept the stressor. There are situations that cannot be controlled. Accepting the stressor can reduce its impact.

Researchers have found the following activities reduce stress significantly:

- Meditating
- Listening to music
- Getting enough sleep
- Drinking black tea
- Spending time with a friend
- Doing something spiritual
- Chewing gum

Other ways to reduce stress might include:
- Exercising
- Developing good time management skills
- Eating a healthy diet
- Organization such as keeping workspace organized
- Picturing yourself relaxed
- Breathing deeply
- Social interaction such as spending time with family and friends
- Positive thinking

Conclusion

Sometimes, stress can be a positive motivator in our lives, but too much stress can create human relations issues, productivity, and other serious health issues. To improve human relations, we need to hone our strengths and weaknesses (self-awareness skills) and understand what human relations skills we should and could improve upon. In those areas we identify as our strengths, we need to continue to develop those strengths. By practicing self-awareness and then self-management, we can begin to realize those things that cause us stress and deal with them in a healthier manner.

The greatest mistake we make while building relationships; is we listen only the half, understand the quarter, and think almost nothing but react double.

R. K. Mohapatra's Award-Winning and Bestselling Books

Investment Risk & Growth
A Guide for Investor
About Investment Vehicles

There is no definite way to educate others about investment products and their return which is widely available in the market. It varies from person to person, place to place, and market to market. Each of us will draw different approaches and gateways to begin our personal financial planning consciously and unconsciously.

We also sometimes share our views with experienced advisers and get a better experience of ourselves. Even though we may not know all the possibilities of risk and rewards in an investment product, we believe in certain philosophies and principles of our economy and try to utilize our hard-earned money in this market in the best ways. We always prefer to invest in less risky assets, as it is human behavior to work in a comfort zone. Return on investment cannot beat inflation with the involvement of risk. You must acquire financial knowledge and faith in the best products by evaluating the investment's pros and cons and setting your financial goal in the long run.

This book, *"Investment Risk & Growth—A Guide for Investors about Investment Vehicles"*, enables an idea about the investments, financial goals, and investment products available in the market.

This book describes the financial planning for individuals and the future growth of financial products in India. You can get your desired goal by making a road map of your investment and choosing the right product at the right time and place. This book consists of six chapters along with examples to reflect an investor's perspective on carefully handling his or her hard-earned money through proper investment planning. This book is meant to enlighten readers on how to invest, what to invest, and where to start.

Notable Author Mohapatra has won the prestigious book award for the 2020 Reader's Favourite – Gold Medal for his bestselling book, Investment Risk & Growth: A Guide for Investors about Investment Vehicles."

Praise for "Investment Risk & Growth: A Guide for Investors about Investment Vehicles"

'This book enlightens readers about the varied aspects of investment coupled with what to invest, and when to make the right started. The book presents a practical evaluation as well as a systematic study of investment products. Plaudits to Mohapatra for demonstrating how easy and uncomplicated it is to get the desired return in uncertain market which hidden truths nowadays, and also discovers a world where investment shows the way to achieve the desired goal of an individual in the long-run. This book empowers the reader's vis-à-vis, the investments and investment products along with financial planning, strategy, insurance and taxation laws.'

—Dr. D.K. Batra,
Eminent Academician and Management Consultant

"R K Mohapatra, from Ircon International Ltd, New Delhi, in a meticulous introduction running into 70 pages describes the topic of financial planning for an individual along with future growth of financial product in India and the title of his work 'Investment Risk & Growth-A guide for investors about investment vehicles'.

—Hindustan Times, New Delhi, May 14, 2013.

"This book is meant to enlighten readers on how to invest, in what to invest, and where to get started. The author forecasts the growth of gold based on the past 10 years' data, which will definitely help readers invest in gold and snatch the benefit of gold and diversify portfolios."

—Early Times Plus, Jammu, July 29, 2013.

THINK FOR FUTURE,
THINK OF RETIREMENT!

R. K. Mohapatra's award-winning book, "Retirement Planning: A Simple Guide for Individuals", deals with retirement planning for individuals vis-a-vis reflects the growth potential of financial products in India. "Retirement Planning: A Simple Guide for Individuals" uses concise and concrete examples to help you better understand the pre-retirement stage (accumulation period), preservation stage, and post-retirement stage (distribution period).

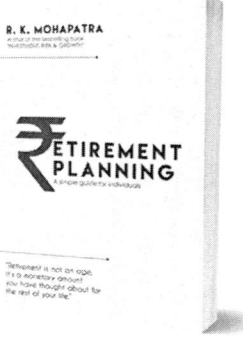

You can get your desired goal by making a retirement road map by choosing the right product at the right time and place.

This book helps you take meaningful decisions for your retirement, whether you are thirty or fifty, and guides you to develop an attitude and aptitude for the habit of saving for retirement and other financial goals.

This global bestseller has been reviewed by

Dr. Ashish Kumar Sana, Professor, Department of Commerce, University of Calcutta, in "The Management Accountant, December 2016", a leading journal of the ICAI, and by Gisela Dixon for Reader's Favorite as well on e-media the world over.

"Retirement Planning- A Simple Guide for Individuals" enlightens readers, especially the middle class, on how to invest, instruments in which to invest, and where to get started. This book is available on Amazon, Flipkart, Shopclues, and Blue Rose publishers under the category of non-fiction business self-help.

Praise for

"Retirement Planning
A Simple Guide for Individuals"

Financial expert R. K. Mohapatra launched his new book titled 'Retirement Planning' on June 8, 2016, by presenting a copy of the book to Dr. Mahesh Sharma, Minister of State (Independent charge) Culture & Tourism and Civil Aviation. The Minister while lauding the painstaking efforts of the author, emphasized the relevance of being mentally prepared for the inevitable retirement stage of life so as to efficiently plan the future.

In the book, author Mohapatra has elaborately explained with well-researched analysis and analytical calculation on how to accumulate retirement corpus during the pre-retirement period besides educating readers about ways to preserve the accumulated corpus during the preservation stage, and thus get the desired post-retirement expenses during the distribution stage.

Besides his financial acumen, the accomplished author is also a philanthropist and an activist in his own right and this is what sets him apart. Despite a hectic work schedule where he has to adhere to stringent deadlines and targets, Mohapatra has effectively managed time to pursue his passion for authoring books on relevant financial matters pertaining to the problems and queries of the common man. It was his deep-rooted interest coupled with his profound knowledge on diverse subjects such as financial planning, budget, Insurance, Will, Digital India Campaign, GST Bill, provident fund, mutual funds, economic reforms, taxation, etc that inspired Mohapatra to wear the hat of an 'author'.

Mohapatra feels that authors render a great service to humanity when they are able to impart and share their vast knowledge and sustainable solutions with masses.

A good author according to him is one who knows how to astutely convey the larger than life message through their books. Whether directly or indirectly, the books should be embedded with a theme that can sustain itself over generations so that they don't become obsolete with the passage of time."

—*Tennews.in, New Delhi, Noida & Greater Noida*

"Financial expert R K Mohapatra, from Ircon International Ltd, recently won the Eminent Author award at the 32nd Dr. S. Radha Krishnan Memorial National Media Network Awards-2016 for his meticulous introduction running into 252 pages of the bestselling book, "Retirement Planning-A simple guide for individuals" from Chief Guest, Sh. Ram Niwas Goel, Hon'ble Speaker Delhi Vidhan Sabha, Noted educationist Dayanand Vats, General Secretary, Akhil Bhartiya Swatantra PatrakarAvomLekhak Sangh."

—*Active Times, Mumbai*

"Financial expert RK Mohapatra recently launched his new book titled "Retirement Planning" by presenting a copy of the book to Dr. Mahesh Sharma, Minister of State (Independent charge) Culture & Tourism and Civil Aviation. The Minister lauded the meticulous efforts of the young author and spoke on the relevance of being mentally prepared for the retirement stage of life from an early stage of the career. The book reflects and focuses on an individual's retirement need, corpus for retirement, and use of created corpus after the superannuation."

—*Trade Reporter*

"The biggest fear for a large part of population about retirement is its ability to maintain the current lifestyle post-retirement. The book, "Retirement Planning" is a simple guide for individuals that describes the topic of retirement planning for individuals along with future growth of financial products in India."

—*The Free Press Journal since 1928, Mumbai*

The book describes the topic of retirement planning for individuals along with future growth of financial products in India, which was published by Blue Rose Publishers, reflects and focuses on an individual's retirement needs, corpus for retirement, and use of created corpus after the superannuation.

—*Mumbai Lakhshadeep*

Reviewed by Gisela Dixon for Readers Favorite

Retirement Planning: A Simple Guide for Individuals by RK Mohapatra is a good book on retirement strategies and planning, along with solid financial management tips. Retirement Planning is specifically written for investors and people who would be investing in India.

The book is divided into several chapters on topics including budgeting, importance of long-term financial planning, meaning of basic financial tools and terminologies, mutual funds and expense ratios, stocks, commonly used financial indexes and benchmarks (Sharpe ratio, alpha, beta, etc.), calculation of interest vs. inflation, insurance, as well as information on specific funds in India such as PPF. All of this and more is divided neatly into chapters so that information is easy to find and well categorized.

This is an excellent book on individual and personal financial planning. What I really liked about the book is the manner in which terms and strategies are simply explained so that they can be easily understood by a layperson. Another huge advantage is the real examples and analyses provided throughout the book that show how to calculate expenses vs interest rates over different periods of time for different funds.

All of the examples and information are based on Indian government rates and funds available in India. However, for a person investing elsewhere, this is still an excellent insight into overall retirement planning and strategies as the basic principles remain the same. An excellent book written in a very easy to understand manner that I would recommend to readers of any age.

It is never too early to start saving.

CMA Rabindra Kumar Mohapatra (R K Mohapatra) is a blogger, speaker, writer, social activist, and award-winning bestselling author. He is known for his work on cash and wealth management, portfolio analysis, financial planning, and retirement planning.

He is a very successful and renowned Indian author in the field of non-fiction self-help books worldwide.

R K Mohapatra (born 1963), MBA/Finance, FCMA, with rich 32 years of experience in the field of finance in India and abroad, is now working as General Manager of Finance at the IRCON INTERNATIONAL LTD.

He has authored four books, "Retirement Planning: A Simple Guide for Individuals," "Investment Risk & Growth: A Guide for Investors about Investment Vehicles," "Sahi Nivesh Se Ameer Banen (Hindi Edition)" and "Mutual Funds: A Powerful Investment Avenue for Individuals."

He is very organized and practical on the topic of personal finance, budget estimate, retirement plan, and mutual fund investment. Mohapatra's honest and striking portrayals of the corporate world earned him numerous national and international awards and exceptional caliber in the world of finance.

R K Mohapatra was honored with the "IRCON Managing Director award" in 1999-2000 for his remarkable contribution to IRCON. His contribution to social and religious fields is also commendable, in addition to his work related to finance and accounts. He was also honored as an activist by the Kalagul Shaktipeeth Mandir, Trust, Sylhet, in the year 2008 for his philanthropic efforts and great initiatives on social work at Shaktipeeth, Maa Kalagul Temple, Sylhet, Bangladesh.

R K Mohapatra won the eminent author award at the 32nd Dr. S. Radha Krishnan Memorial, National Media Network Awards-2016 for his meticulous bestselling book, "Retirement Planning - A Simple Guide for Individuals."

CMA R K Mohapatra was nominated for "CMA – Achiever Awards" in 2017. Financial expert R K Mohapatra has been honored with the prestigious Exemplary Leader Award 2019 at the 18th edition of the Asia Pacific HRM Congress.

R K Mohapatra's third book, "Mutual funds: A powerful investment Avenue for Individuals," won the Literary Titan Gold Book Award 2020 in the USA.

Notable Author R K Mohapatra has won the prestigious book

R K Mohapatra rewarded Eminent Author Awards

award for the 2020 Reader's Favourite – Gold Medal for his bestselling book, "Investment Risk & Growth: A Guide for Investors about Investment Vehicles."

R K Mohapatra, GM/Finance, IRCON, has been conferred "Hall of Fame," 19th Edition Asian HR Leadership Awards 2021

in the excellence of Individuals category, of his remarkable contributions to IRCON and exceptional caliber to the world of finance.

Cherry Book Awards- Guest of Honour-2021.

Mohapatra was awarded the Best Seller BLUE ROSE Book Awards 2021 for his book "Retirement Planning: A Simple Guide for Individuals" and "Mutual funds: A Powerful Investment Avenue for Individuals."

Mohapatra has been nominated as Finalist Author at NE8x Online Litfest 2021 edition for his exemplary contribution to non-fiction best-selling book, "Mutual funds: A Powerful Investment Ivestment Avenue for Individuals."

For sheer outstanding talent and impressive writing skills, Mohapatra has been honored with the Criticspace Literary Awards' Best Indian Author Awards – 2021.

R K Mohapatra, honored as "Inspiring Indian 2022" for his contribution across talent domains, striving for excellence in genres across the nation and beyond.

Recently, the global foundation honored R K Mohapatra with the super prestigious "Bhartiya Sahitya Ratna- Best Author Award-2022" in recognition of his immense contribution to literature across talent domains, striving for excellence in genres across the nation and beyond.

The reasons why many of his friends and colleagues refer to him as a "Philanthropist" is because he has always been there to offer his expert advice to all those who come to seek his opinion on financial issues sans any tantrums.

A good author according to him is the one who knows how to astutely convey the larger than life message through his books, whether directly or indirectly; the book should be embedded with a theme that can sustain itself over generations so that they don't become obsolete with the passage of time.

The author is passionate about writing on several platforms, articles on financial matters in newspapers, magazines, and blogs, and spreading knowledge through online media.

R K Mohapatra is the cover star of "SELFESTA," "PANDORA," AND "GLORIOUS INDIA" Magazines and a multitalented personality, has been interviewed in many media houses: The Free Press Journal, TheIndiestimes.com, JNews, Hitimes, Books & Author Bulletin, The Literature Today, Criticspace, Literary Titan, PressReader, There and Their and Including The magazine of Selfesta, Passion Review, and Glorious India.

Financial Expert R K Mohapatra was a speaker and panelist on the theme: "SHAPE OF THINGS TO COME...." at the

18th Edition Asia Pacific HRM Congress, Taj Yeshwantpur, Bangalore, and Chief speaker on the topic "Investment Opportunity and Risk Management in India" at ICAI, Bhubaneswar Chapter, Bhubaneswar, in 2019. He was also one of the speakers on the Topic "Smart Investment for a Secure Retirement" in a webinar organized by Moneycontrol.com and sponsored by Bajaj Alliance in Jan 2021.

The author always welcomes readers to provide their valuable suggestions and comments.

Readers may connect the author at: www.rabindramohapatra.com, www.rkmohapatra.com,

or rk.mohapatra.as@gmail.com and on social media: Facebook, LinkedIn, Twitter, Instagram & Pinterest.